THE
BALANCE EQUATION

Self + Health + Relationships + Money

Find Your Formula for Living Your Best Life

ROB FIANCE

AND

STUART ROSENBLUM

BEACHFRONT PUBLISHING | WESLAKE VILLAGE, CA

Published by
Beachfront Publishing | Westlake, CA

Publisher's Cataloging-in-Publication Data

Fiance, Rob.

The balance equation : find your formula for living your best life / Rob Fiance and Stuart Rosenblum. – Westlake Village, CA : Beachfront Pub., 2022.

p. ; cm.

ISBN13: 978-0-9601169-0-4

1. Life skills. 2. Self-actualization (Psychology). 3. Health. 4. Interpersonal relations. 5. Finance, Personal. I. Title. II. Rosenblum, Stuart.

HQ2037.F53 2022
646.7--dc23

Printed in the United States of America

26   25   24   23   22   •   5   4   3   2   1

For our awesome families, the Rosenblums (Andrea, Andrew, Garrett, Abby, Amy, Virginia, and Wesley) and the Fiances (Beth, Alex, Jeremy, Talia, Kelly, and Ruby), and a big thank you to our dads for teaching us to save by paying ourselves first.

Contents

Preface

It was a beautiful, sunny summer Saturday morning. Stu and Rob were at a seaside resort in Santa Barbara, California, recovering from the previous night's pre-wedding costume disco party celebration with family and friends. This was the first of many events that weekend devoted to celebrating the wedding of Alex and Kelly, Rob's son and new daughter. We both independently picked up a copy of the *Wall Street Journal*. Thumbing through the pages, we read the shocking headline: "Anthony Bourdain, Chef and CNN Host, Dead at 61." Immediately, we texted each other. Bourdain had died by suicide on location in France for *Parts Unknown*. How could this have happened to a guy who seemingly had it all?

We had felt connected to Bourdain. Close to our age, he had made a hugely successful career out of food, travel, and above all connecting with people from all walks of life. What shocked us most was his response to a question about balance and the notion of stepping back from the breakneck pace of a job that had kept him on the road 250 days a year: "Too late for that. I think about it. I aspired to it. I feel guilty about it. I yearn for it. Balance? I fu*king wish."

Stunned by Bourdain's suicide, we got together that afternoon and realized we needed to accelerate our commitment to writing this book. If we could help one person feel better about life, then maybe we could save them from taking their life.

We asked ourselves how we felt about our own lives and compared notes. We both felt good about some areas and not so good about others. We each had a system and tools that helped us track specific components of our lives, but neither of us had found a complete program. Thus, we decided to develop the formula for living our—and your—best life. Our hope is that *The Balance Equation™: Find Your Formula for Living Your Best Life* will help you to do just that.

—Rob and Stu

Introduction

This book focuses on how to accomplish the things that are important to you that seldom or never actually happen.

We all fall out of balance; it's the nature of our busy lifestyles. People who are determined to live their best lives through family and friends, careers, hobbies, side hustles, and life in general often struggle the most with balance. As a result, everyone, anyone, and everything else takes priority. How do you prioritize yourself? What are the signs that you're falling out of balance? Here are a few clues:

- You feel more stressed than normal.
- You're short with people at work.
- You don't say goodbye or kiss loved ones when you leave for work.
- You haven't exercised or even moved in weeks.
- You're overspending.
- You're always looking at your phone, even when someone is sitting across from you.
- You struggle to stay present with people.
- You're overeating, undereating, or, worse, not eating at all.
- You have a habit of not returning phone calls or texts.
- You haven't taken a vacation or long weekend in years.
- You feel defensive when people talk about the things they enjoy.
- You find it challenging to be happy for other people's success.

The list goes on . . .

There is no silver bullet, short cut, or quick fix to these problems. You can't buy a great life; you must work to create it. You are not alone, as most of us are dealing with many of the same issues. We are constantly barraged with advertisements, podcasts, books, articles, and other messages that promise a better life, health, longevity, relationships, wealth, etc., for just a few easy payments. *Like you, we are tired of all the BS.*

We continue to be haunted by the words of Anthony Bourdain: "Balance? I f*cking wish." He knew he needed to change but was unable to do so.

Don't fall into that trap. We can *all* change, but it takes work. It takes time to live your priorities and feel good about your life. But unless you have a system to follow, it's difficult to make the time to make the changes.

Steve Jobs, who died way too soon, shared his thoughts about our limited time and living our best lives: "Remembering that I'll be dead soon is the most important tool I've ever encountered to help me make the big choices in life. Because almost everything—all external expectations, all pride, all fear of embarrassment or failure—these things just fall away in the face of death, leaving only what is truly important."

Many years before the two of us met, we both struggled to balance our lives. Neither of us was happy with the way things were going, and we both felt out of control. Though certain individual experiences were similar, some were quite different. We both were managing young families with wives who were full-time mothers to three children close in ages. We both were workaholics who thought money would solve everything. What was different was how the stress of being out of control showed up.

Stu's rock bottom arrived in his late forties. His finances were in shambles, his marriage was challenged, his health was bad (he was more than one hundred pounds overweight), he had no time for himself, and he felt like a total loser. Stu described his feelings at the time as follows:

"I always felt on the edge, putting one fire out after another, with no time to breathe. Everyone was disappointed, including me."

After many attempts to solve these issues on his own, all of which failed, Stu took a step back and assessed each area of his life. He discovered he needed to work on himself, and he did. Change was difficult, but he established a morning routine that began with planning and reflection. Today, he utilizes the Balance Equation™ in all aspects of his life. More than eighty pounds lighter, he's been happily married for more than thirty-four years, all three of his kids are college graduates and making their own way in the world, and his finances continue to grow while he thrives in his senior executive role at a Fortune 20 company. While Stu has made great progress, he continues to work on improving his balance each and every day.

Rob hit rock bottom in his mid-thirties when he found himself under the spell of chasing financial independence that resulted in sixty-to-eighty-hour work weeks plus long commute times. His lack of sleep, excessive stress, chronic indigestion and depression, and little time for his loved ones was definitely taking its toll. Rob's turning point and "Aha" moment came when his wife, Beth, asked him, "Why are you always bragging about how many hours you work? Do you think that's something to be proud of?" Rob recalls, "I'd never thought about this so clearly before, as work ethic was so deeply ingrained in my family."

Rob described his feelings at the time as follows: "I was overworked. It was 'Same sh*t, different day' on autopilot. I wasn't enjoying my life with the people I love. I felt like a failure and knew things needed to change."

He tried all sorts of quick fixes, books, tapes, meditations, you name it. Nothing worked. Progress came from a personal retreat where he did some soul searching and started tracking the hours spent in various areas of his life. By committing to the tracking process, he became conscious of where he spent his time, which allowed him to make the adjustments based on his priorities. It wasn't easy, but the time he invested was well worth it. Rob found that he gained two hours per day, ten hours each week. He accomplished this by leaving both the house and the office earlier each day, reducing the number of meetings he attended, reducing the office chit chat, and blocking time for important projects.

The time he gained, he shifted to himself, family, friends, and fun. Living his life based upon his new priorities allowed the stress and negativity to disappear. Today Rob utilizes the Balance Equation™ in all aspects of his life. Happily married for more than thirty-six years, he has three successful adult children, one grandchild, and is a partner in a thriving EdTech company. He feels less overworked and continues to manage the daily struggle of enjoying a balanced life.

We met more than twenty years ago when our kids played youth sports. Over the years at practices or team events, we often talked about business and family, which resulted in mutual respect and a genuine connection. As more time passed, our wives became good friends and we saw each other more frequently. We realized our acquaintance had become a genuine friendship and our discussions became more specific. Eventually, we shared our mutual frustrations revolving around the desire to find time to create lives that were more meaningful.

We have both been advisors to business owners, executives, managers, and others on business matters and many life issues in a variety of industries. We have coached hundreds of kids through youth and high school sports programs. This involvement has given us vast experience and understanding of the challenges people face in trying to balance their lives. Additionally, we've spent many years practicing balance and researching the topic. We believed that life had more to offer, and we were determined to experience it for ourselves and offer the opportunity to others to be more successful at seeking balance as well.

Despite more than four years of research, we couldn't find any programs that clearly addressed how people could assess and improve the balance in their lives. We thought we would have more luck looking for a formula to achieve balance in a corporate setting. Again, nothing. Finally, we searched for a feasible method that could balance both our individual and work lives and combine the two in a way that would encourage and lead to health and happiness. Needless to say, it was strike three. We truly believed our families, friends, and coworkers were facing similar struggles, yet programs balancing wellness and corporate productivity were nonexistent. Consequently, we developed the Balance Equation™, often referred to as TBE. This is a complete program designed to focus on all of the categories in one's life in entirety and to help people develop their own plan for living their best and most balanced life.

We all have our own ideas of what it means to live a balanced life, and we all have different circumstances. What we hone in on in *The Balance Equation™: Find Your Formula for Living Your Best Life* is how we feel about the lives we are living and whether or not we are focused on what is most important to us.

We define balance as *living a life where all your priorities are reflected by the way you spend your time.* There is no such thing as perfect balance, but finding your balance is entirely doable. A great example of a life well lived by someone who has found her balance is Stu's Aunt Gertie, who lived to be 104 years old.

We both want to be like Aunt Gertie when we grow up. We recently asked her to share her secrets for a long and fulfilling life. Here is her response:

1. Have a positive attitude and don't sweat the small stuff.
2. Spend time with people and have positive interactions.
3. Keep moving every day.
4. Continue to use your mind through reading and conversation.
5. Get the right amount of sleep.

AUNT GERTIE & STU
at her 104ᵗʰ Birthday Celebration

Research confirms that Aunt Gertie's secrets to a long life are consistent with the secrets of many others who have reached their one hundred-plus milestone. While we don't know how long we will live, we do know that we want to live the remainder of our lives as happily as Aunt Gertie. We want you to feel good about your life too.

This book concentrates on what we have control over, such as our mindset, work ethic, nutrition, exercise, and the way we treat others. Of course, we recognize there are other factors that we have no control over such as natural disasters, illness, death, and other people's actions. Sh*t happens. But hopefully, as your mind and body become more balanced, your coping mechanisms and resiliency will improve. A small change today—what we call a Micro-move™ in this book—can have an exponential effect on how your future plays out.

The Balance Equation™ includes exercises, called ● **TBE EXERCISE**, and case studies, called ⫫ **TBE IN ACTION**, to help you practice and see real life examples of the Balance Equation™ in use.

We developed the Balance Equation™ as a simple, comprehensive, hands-on, easy-to-use program to help you live your best life by focusing on your priorities. It has made a difference in our lives and changed them for the better. We now live our priorities and feel better about ourselves and the lives we lead. We are confident this program will help you cultivate your most balanced life, and we welcome you as the newest member of our growing community. So, let's dive in.

Why the Balance Equation™

The key is in not spending time, but in investing it.

—Stephen R. Covey, author

We all have the same 525,600 minutes, 8,760 hours, and 365 days every year to do with as we choose. Remember the song "Seasons of Love" from the show *Rent* that starts with 525,600 minutes? The lyrics are as follows: "How do you measure? Measure a year? In daylights? In sunsets? In midnights? In cups of coffee? In inches? In miles? In laughter? In strife? . . . How do you measure a year in a *life*?"

The way we use our time affects each moment in our journey and ultimately defines the story of our life. Our life story does not end until we are out of time. Knowing how we spend our time will allow us to evaluate where we are on our journey.

Everyone uses one hundred percent of their time every day. How that time is spent is up to the individual. Whether we are staring into space, sleeping, exercising, working, talking on the phone, binge watching, arguing, worrying, loving, praying, eating, or anything else, each of us chooses and controls our time.

To make changes in anything you do, you must have a clear understanding of your starting point, of the real story, not the BS so many of us tell ourselves. So how do you do this? It starts with knowing your current state, or how you feel about your life today. Knowing your current state will give you clarity about what you need to change to achieve your desired future state.

In other words, nothing can get better until you have a clear picture of how you feel about your situation right now. If you are unhappy where you are today, life will not change unless and until you take an action to do something different. You need to not only *want* to change but also be *willing* to change while feeling sufficiently *safe* to change. Ask yourself:

- Am I living the vision I have for myself?
- Am I living my goals?
- Do I have a clear picture of where I am in my life?
- Do I allow myself to feel my feelings?
- Why do I feel the way I do?

- Do I care enough for myself?
- How is my health?
- How much time do I spend on or at work?
- Do I love my profession?
- Is how I spend my time in line with who I am and who I want to be?
- Do I spend enough time nurturing my relationships?
- Are there things I want to do that I am unable to fit into my life?
- What are my priorities?
- Do I believe that money would solve all my problems?
- Do I say "yes" to everything?
- Are there enough hours in the day to get it all done?
- Am I conscious of where my time goes?
- Am I in jeopardy of losing everything?

If any of these questions resonate with you, the Balance Equation™ program can add great value to your life.

The Balance Equation™ Community

We created the Balance Equation™ Community to provide a safe space for shared experiences, best practices, and ongoing support for our members. Being part of a community, whether physical or virtual, gives people the chance to be inspired, solve problems, share achievements, and vent frustrations while laughing and crying together. Community is helpful for many but not for everyone, and you can join at any time by signing up at TheBalanceEquation.com or using the QR code below.

Open up the camera on your phone and scan the QR code, which will bring you to a menu. Click on "Get Your Balance Number Now!" to take the assessment.

Measure to Change

"What gets measured gets done." This quote comes from management guru Peter Drucker, who likewise said, "What gets measured gets managed."

The basic concept explains that if you measure something you want to change, the probability that you will achieve change is a lot higher. While this notion is a business concept, it also applies to our personal lives. Regular measurement and reporting will keep you focused on what you're trying to achieve and will create a cycle of continuous improvement. All of us will struggle at different points in our lives. When this happens to you, focus on changing one thing at a time.

The 2011 movie *Moneyball* depicts actor Brad Pitt as a baseball general manager who turns around the Oakland Athletics baseball team and improves their chances of winning games. The movie is based on the story of Billy Beane, a general manager of the A's. His assistant, a young economics graduate student, uses statistics to convert Oakland's failing baseball team into one of the most successful and winningest franchises of all time. Likewise, measuring is at the heart of the Balance Equation™.

How Does the Balance Equation™ Work?

The Balance Equation™ is comprised of four categories and twenty subcategories that help you determine how you feel about all the areas of your life at any given moment. Everyone talks about wanting balance, which is why phrases like "work-life balance," "balanced diet," or "financial balance" are routinely thrown around. But when it's all said and done, balance comes down to how you spend your time, who you spend it with, and where and when you spend it.

Each of us has the exact same amount of time. As previously discussed, we each have one hundred percent control over how we decide to use our time, and we all make different choices. To examine how you are spending your time, ask yourself the following questions:

- Are you mindful of how you use your time or are you on autopilot and just going through the motions?
- When you want to do something new, do you add it on to everything that you're already doing?
- Do you realize that when you add something new, like a yoga class, helping a friend, or volunteering, you must subtract something else, like playing with your kids, watching TV, or even sleeping?

The Balance Equation™ process, illustrated in the graphic on the next page, is simple: take a quick assessment to see your life balance, reflect on your assessment results and where you want to feel better, prioritize the categories you want to improve by choosing one or more Micro-moves™ that allow you to optimize your choices, and thus the growth and improvement cycle begins. While everyone's situation is different, the Balance Equation™ is your unique personal tool for gaining clarity on how you're doing in these various aspects of your life.

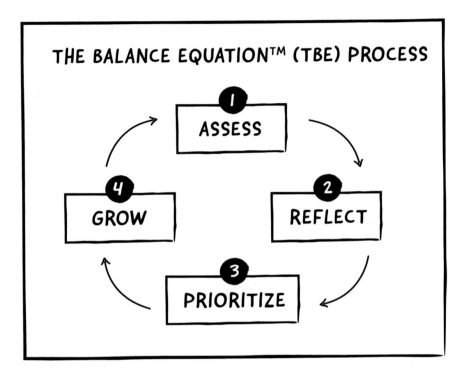

1. **Assess:** take a quick assessment to see how you currently feel about your life balance.
2. **Reflect:** think about the results of your assessment and the categories you want to feel better about.
3. **Prioritize:** choose the category or categories you want to feel better about and the Micro-moves™ to help you change.
4. **Grow:** the compounding impact of assessing, reflecting, and prioritizing will fuel your continued growth and improvement.

Once you've completed the four steps, you basically rinse and repeat because achieving balance is an ongoing process.

The Four Categories of the Balance Equation™

The Balance Equation™ applies these four steps—assess, reflect, prioritize, grow—to four important life categories: self, health, relationships, and money. The equation looks like this:

The Balance Equation™ = Self + Health + Relationships + Money

Within these four categories are twenty subcategories:

SELF	RELATIONSHIPS
Core values and beliefs	Most significant other
Personal time	Family
Development	Friends
Work	Work
Spiritual	Inner circle

HEALTH	MONEY
Physical	Basic expenses
Mental	Debt
Emotional	Savings
Food	Retirement
Sleep	Charity

It's All About the Math

The Balance Equation™ helps to quantify where we spend our time and how we balance it all. Naturally, everyone's Balance Equation™ is unique. The amount of time we spend working, sleeping, or engaged in any particular activity varies. The one thing everyone has in common is the opportunity to choose how they spend their finite time. How we spend it should be up to us, or at least mostly up to us. The "balance" comes in how we move and navigate through the different areas.

For example, think about how much time you spend exercising. A lot? A little? Not at all? To some people, exercise is discretionary. To others, it's mandatory. As you think about your day, identify categories that are mandatory versus discretionary, negotiable versus non-negotiable, and why each category is or is not important to you.

The Balance Equation™ calculates numbers—twenty in total—that reflect how you feel overall and in the four major categories of life at a specific, given point in time. There are no good or bad numbers, and they are always evolving. Perfect balance isn't attainable, but it is a goal to strive for. We are all unique, and therefore we all have a different Balance Equation™.

Once your assessment is complete and you have received your numbers, it's important to think about the areas in your life that you want to improve. In the TBE process, we refer to this as the reflect stage. It is crucial to be honest and ask yourself, "Do I want to improve some of the categories that I gave the lowest scores to?" If the answer is yes, then it will make sense to start with the one that is causing you the most pain and frustration.

Man Plans and God Laughs

Rob fondly remembers his grandparents and dad saying in Yiddish, "Mann tracht, und Gott lacht," which means "Man plans and God laughs." In other words, expect the unexpected. Unplanned things happen. Along the same lines, former heavyweight boxing champion Mike Tyson once said, "Everyone has a plan until they get punched in the face." Whether the loss of loved ones (perhaps from suicide, a heart attack, or a drug overdose), a cancer diagnosis, the loss of a boss, the loss of a job, or financial losses, we have all experienced unplanned events throughout our lives.

When unexpected things happen, practice self-compassion, take whatever time you need to adjust, and then get back to your Balance Equation™ routines—something we'll discuss shortly—as soon as possible.

 **TBE EXERCISE**

Assess Where You Are Right Now

To determine where you stand right now, click on the QR code below. It will only take a few minutes to do the assessment, and it will position you to begin making important changes in your life.

 Open up the camera on your phone and scan the QR code which will bring you to a menu. Click on "Get Your Balance Number Now!" to take the assessment.

RECAP

We developed the Balance Equation™ knowing that what we measure, we can change. We wanted to develop a program that would help us and others improve their lives. It all begins with assessing how you feel about all aspects of your life. Once you know where you stand, you're in a position to identify the areas you need to work on.

The Balance Equation™ program offers a simple, four-step process for continuous growth:

1. **Assess:** take a quick assessment to see how you currently feel about your life balance.
2. **Reflect:** think about the results of your assessment results and the categories where you want to feel better.
3. **Prioritize:** choose the category or categories you want to feel better about and the Micro-moves™ to help you change.
4. **Grow:** the compounding of assessment, reflection, and prioritization will fuel your continued growth.

Then rinse and repeat by going back to assess. We know that achieving balance is an ongoing process.

Again, there is no such thing as perfect balance in life, but finding *your* balance is totally doable and utterly worth it. There will always be areas that need work; balance comes from working on all areas of your life. Given that we are all works in progress, here are some thoughts to consider:

- Our definition of balance means living a life where all our priorities are reflected by the way that we spend our time.
- Define what balance means to you and your life.

- Are you living your life focused on the things that are truly most important to you?
- The results of your assessment will identify areas for you to consider prioritizing.
- Sh*t happens. Expect the unexpected.

In the next chapter, you will learn why your assessment number is crucial and the vitally important benefits of something we call Micro-moves™.

An Introduction to Micro-moves™

The Balance Equation™ = Self + Health + Relationships + Money

Balance is not something you find—it is something you create.

—Jana Kingsford

By now, you've taken the assessment and established your overall Balance Equation™ number. We call this your TBE number. It's important because it helps you understand the whole picture of you.

Digging in more deeply, you've learned your number in each of the four Balance Equation™ categories and now have a handle on how you're doing in those specific areas of your life. We chose smiley faces and the corresponding five-point scale shown below so you can easily reflect on how you feel about each area of your life at any given time. Let's look at this scale a bit more closely.

TBE FEELINGS SCALE

 1. When you give yourself a 1, you are really struggling in this category. Feelings are at their lowest point.

2. When you give yourself a 2, you are still struggling in this category at this time, but you are not at your lowest point.

 3. When you give yourself a 3, you don't feel your best but you don't believe you are struggling. This category, in the middle of the road, reveals an attitude of "meh."

 4. When you give yourself a 4, you feel good about the category and your present state even though you aren't yet at your best.

5. When you give yourself a 5, you feel your absolute best about this category and are supremely happy with your current state.

Which smiley face and corresponding number do you choose for each area of your life? The answer provides a snapshot of where you are at this given moment. If you take the same assessment tomorrow, your TBE number may be different. By understanding where you stand by assessing your number today, no matter which area of your life needs change or is out of balance, you can make it better one Micro-move™ at a time.

☝ INTRODUCING MICRO-MOVES™

Micro-moves™ are small changes that allow you to immediately begin addressing the areas in your life that you want to feel better about. These small personal changes give you movement in a positive direction. As Vincent van Gogh said, "Great things are done by a series of small things brought together."

Don't feel overwhelmed or think you need to change everything at once. If you're completely honest, where you are today didn't just randomly happen. Unique circumstances brought you to this place. It will take time to change and improve your circumstances, but it is possible to begin making meaningful efforts today.

We used the word "micro," which means "smaller," to give you, and every move you make, a greater chance of success while building momentum that compounds one success on top of another. The ultimate success of a Micro-move™ is to have it consistently endure and become a habit. The more you make what is important to you habitual, the greater its chance for success.

Most people are so busy that they can't imagine adding something more to their daily schedule, but it is possible by starting small and making this new behavior a priority. For example, you may wish you could read more. You can do that through a Micro-move™ such as committing to reading five minutes a day. Grab that book you've always wanted to read, set the timer, and do it. You will be amazed at how many books you can read in a year with this simple Micro-move™.

If you need to incorporate exercise into your life, do push-ups or air squats in the kitchen while the microwave heats your morning beverage. Keep dumbbells near your desk, and when you take a break from the computer, do a set of curls. Mindfully get up from your desk and walk around your office or take a stroll around the block once or twice a day.

These Micro-moves™ prove that you don't have to make drastic changes in order to see improvement in a specific area of your life. You don't have to wait a long time before you start seeing positive results, either. All you have to do is take small steps consistently, and before long, they will become powerful daily habits.

The truth is most self-improvement programs don't work because they take a one-size-fits-all approach without considering specific circumstances and individual personalities. Instead, the Balance Equation™ encourages you to make personalized Micro-moves™. Micro-moves that result in changes and that help you achieve your goals will no doubt start you on the road to living your best life.

One of the most important aspects of Micro-moves™ is that they allow you to make positive adjustments without a huge drain of time. They fit into your life with minimal effort and disruption of your normal day-to-day activities. Consequently, this gives you the highest probability of success. Based on your priorities, these Micro-moves™ add up quickly to help you feel better and optimize your life.

Develop your own Micro-moves™ or get started by using one or more of the following examples:

1. Write a sentence per day in a journal.
2. Meditate for one minute.

3. Do twenty jumping jacks or pushups while your coffee brews in the morning.
4. Send a quick "thinking of you" text to a special someone or friend.

Each move, while micro, gives you momentum towards living your best life. When you are focused on your priorities and are open towards making progress through Micro-moves™, you are more likely to achieve positive changes in your life.

For example, if improving your health is a priority, then movement or exercise is an integral part of achieving your goal. A corresponding Micro-move™ would be to sign up for a step tracker that automatically tracks your steps.

The key to Micro-moves™ is that they should be small, like drinking a glass of water, to help you gain immediate momentum. Likewise, Micro-moves™ such as waking up ten minutes earlier each day, going to sleep ten minutes earlier, drinking one fewer cup of coffee, or sustaining one minute of meditation are all little moves that help you get to where you want to be, but it bears repeating that you can't do everything at once. If you have a low number in some areas and aren't where you want to be, Micro-moves™ allow you to choose an area to work on. If you have a high number in a category, you probably feel good about that and don't need to work on it now. With the Balance Equation™, you can prioritize what is important to you at any point in time without being overwhelmed. The assessment process carries on as you continue to evaluate areas of your life for ongoing improvement.

☝ TEN MORE EXAMPLES OF MICRO-MOVES™

Additional examples of Micro-moves™ that take a mere thirty seconds to two minutes include the following:

1. Make a list of the things you enjoy doing but don't seem to have time for.
2. Stop reading this book and go for a walk.
3. Eat lunch outdoors.
4. Remove the excess clutter from your desk.
5. Stand up from your chair and do some stretching exercises.
6. Download an app that helps you track your spending for the week.
7. Choose one credit card and commit to paying it down.
8. Schedule time for self-care (take a longer shower or nap).
9. Start meditating.
10. Send someone who needs encouragement a thoughtful text.

Your TBE Number Right Now

If you've already taken the assessment, you're aware of your overall current TBE number. If it's in the mid-seventies, there are areas in your life that you feel need improvement. Perhaps you need to work on your health, make more time for your relationships, spend time working on your finances, or simply make time for *you*. It all comes back to your priorities. Again, ask yourself:

- Where do I want to be?
- Where am I now?
- How do I improve?
- How do I prioritize my life?

The Balance Equation™ is your complete picture, the snapshot of the whole you. You must know where you stand before you can improve and design your ideal life. "Balance" has different meanings for each of us, but there are some universal truths. For some, balance means a healthy work-life balance while others believe their minds, bodies, and souls must be in balance. Balance is personal, but too many of us are out of balance, putting things that aren't as important first or letting them tip the scales too far in one direction. We have learned the importance of balance in our lives, and hopefully this book will inspire you to find balance in yours.

 # TBE EXERCISE

Design Your Ideal Day
If you could create your ideal schedule for a day, what would it look like?

- What would you want to do?
- What would you want to eat?
- Who would you want to see?
- Would you sleep in?
- Would you exercise?
- Would you go to the beach?
- Would you read a book?

- Would you binge a favorite show or see a movie?
- Would work be part of it?
- Would sex be part of it?

The Balance Equation™ allows you to design and manage your ideal life. Once you assess where you are, you're ready to move forward and improve your life.

⃛🏃 TBE IN ACTION

Meet Reid, in College during COVID

Reid Broudy is a college student at the University of Texas Austin who has been using the Balance Equation™ for the past three years. He began the program during the COVID-19 quarantine in 2020 when all his classes went virtual and completed "Zoom University" from his home in California. Reid said, "During this crazy time, my thoughts became a rumble of madness: I had a large to-do list that was hard to make a dent in, I had to keep up with college classes, and I struggled with the realities of not seeing people in person. This difficult search to find balance led me to start using the Balance Equation™."

Reid's first step was to assess his current state by taking the TBE assessment. After receiving his numbers, he took a step back to reflect and soon realized his strength was his health. He said, "It's evident that my workout routine and attention to healthy living has been a large part of my lifestyle. Whether I'm running with my family or doing in-house workouts, I've noticed that exercise not only improves my physical health but also clears my head and positively impacts my mental health."

But not all of Reid's numbers were positive. After taking the TBE assessment, he realized that some of his relationship categories had a lower number. He reflected, "This time in quarantine has allowed me to think about my relationships at a deeper level. I realize now that I'm struggling with the social scene and am having a harder time connecting with my friends."

Reid decided to prioritize relationships and embraced the Micro-move™ of texting his friends more often, especially the ones he couldn't visit in person. His growth came from following the TBE process, not only by adding Micro-moves™ and prioritizing things to do but also by allowing himself to remove items from his list that were no longer a priority. He shared, "I realized it's okay to not clean out every closet or learn a new language. Instead, the pandemic was a time to take a step back and understand that using the time to breathe and reflect was okay."

Checking in with yourself each day can take as little as thirty seconds. Stop right now, take a breath, and think about how you feel. Good? Bad? Meh? Keep it simple; the point is to get in the habit of constantly checking in with yourself and being aware of your feelings.

THE SELF-CHECK-IN MICRO-MOVE™

Do a "self-check-in" when you wake up each morning to see how you feel. By taking a few minutes to do an assessment of all TBE categories, you are allowing yourself to see a complete picture of how you feel and to better prioritize balance in your life.

Taking a self-check-in is something we've been doing consistently as part of our morning routines for more than thirty years. Rob notes, "The simple awareness of how I feel when I wake up sets the tone for how I approach each day. If I feel tired, I might do more meditating. If I feel anxious, I might engage in more affirmations. If I feel lethargic, I might exercise more and get more sleep. If I feel sick, I might focus on eating certain foods and getting more rest. If I don't feel strong, I typically hold off on making important decisions."

RECAP

The Balance Equation™ is made up of four main categories—self, health, relationships, and money—and twenty subcategories, five in each main category. Your number in any of the Balance Equation™ categories reveals how you feel you're doing in each area of your life.

The assessment uses the following scale to make it easy to determine how you feel:

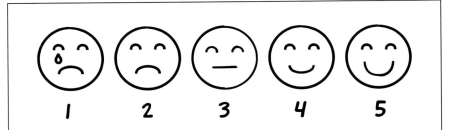

Likewise, we developed the concept of Micro-moves™ to make changes to your life less overwhelming. Engaging in Micro-moves™ gives you a greater chance of success while building momentum that compounds one success on top of another. The ultimate success of a Micro-move™ is that it endures consistently and becomes a habit. The more you make behaviors that are important to you habitual, the greater chance for success.

An integral part of the Balance Equation™ is knowing your total number—the snapshot of the whole you. You learn this number by taking the TBE assessment. If you haven't yet taken the plunge, scan the QR code below and give it a try. Better yet, do it every day so that you can keep your balance and well-being at the forefront and mindfully begin to improve them.

 Open up the camera on your phone and scan the QR code, which will bring you to a menu. Click on "Get Your Balance Number Now!" to take the assessment.

Now that you understand the Balance Equation™ in general, let's dive deeper into the first major category, self.

A Deep Dive into Self

The Balance Equation™ = **Self** + Health + Relationships + Money

*You always have to remember to take care of you first
and foremost, because when you stop taking care of yourself,
you get out of balance, and you really forget how to
take care of others.*

—Jada Pinkett Smith

Self is one of the four main categories of the Balance Equation™. If you don't feel good about yourself, then all the other categories (health, relationships, and money) are affected.

Self = Core Values + Personal Time + Development + Work + Spiritual

Making yourself a priority isn't selfish. On the contrary, it's the most important investment you can make. This includes having a relationship with yourself that continues to evolve. Most of us never slow down enough to ask, "How do I feel about myself?" but that's exactly what we want you to do right now. Look at the five smiley faces in the chart below and answer the question. How do you feel about yourself?

Now take a few moments to reflect on how you feel about your life (this is your self-check-in). Eliminate autopilot by staying conscious about your feelings and thinking deeply about your answer.

One reason you might feel less than thrilled with one or more categories of your life is that you are passing through each day without reflecting or taking the time to think about your priorities. Again, how you spend your time should reflect your priorities. Often, we elevate others' priorities above our own, but it's important to put ourselves first. When we don't, it can lead to resentment that can affect all the categories of the Balance Equation™.

The Balance Equation™ is all about helping you get out of a rut by taking action, but it's also about knowing *why* you're engaging in a particular task.

For example, you might be seeing a personal trainer three times a week. Is that really how you want to spend your time? We all have an idea of what an ideal lifestyle should look like, but the point is to take charge of your life by developing good habits and making Micro-moves™ that are important to you.

Once you truly know what is important for you and you're ready to make a change in your life, make a Micro-move™ to begin that change.

When you take the time to care for yourself, your energy and attitude are healthier and everything in your life improves. Self-care allows you to be your best self. It means you can show up better in all the categories of your life. You might think you don't have time for yourself, but you can make time through Micro-moves™. As mentioned earlier, they allow you to make positive adjustments without a huge drain of time to give you the highest probability of success. As the graphic below proclaims, self-care benefits every category of life.

Research highlights that most people neglect themselves. Many of us are more concerned with pleasing others than with taking time for ourselves, but until you love and care for yourself, you can't optimize your health, take care of your relationships, or think about your finances. With that fact in mind, let's take a closer look at the five subcategories of self, starting with core values:

Self = **Core Values** + Personal Time + Development + Work + Spiritual

Core Values

Did you know that Kobe Bryant gave himself the nickname "the Black Mamba" to help himself get through the lowest point of his career? According to his documentary, *Muse*, he was at the top of his game when he realized he had no idea where his life was going. Creating an alternate persona was his way of mentally moving beyond the struggles he was facing. Kobe had to figure out his core values and deal with the battle raging inside him. Once he did, he was able to get out of his own head and lose the self-doubts that were holding him back. Ultimately, this process became known as the "Mamba Mentality," which is defined as the constant quest to be the best possible version of oneself. Kobe went on to become a great family man, teammate, five-time NBA champion, eighteen-time All-Star, and fourth highest all-time leading scorer. Unfortunately, he and his daughter Gianna were killed in a helicopter crash in Calabasas, California, in 2020.

Do you know your core values? Few of us learn about core values in school. Yes, we saw values modeled by our grandparents, parents, stepparents, aunts, uncles, teachers, clergy, coaches, bosses, and so on, but do you know *your* core values? Core values are the fundamental beliefs we have, the guiding principles that dictate our behavior and decisions and help us understand the difference between right and wrong. Core values can help us determine if we are on the path to fulfilling our goals.

Why is this important? Every day, we make decisions that affect our lives. We need a baseline for our decision making in terms of what is right and wrong so that we know we are making the right decisions for us. All of our behaviors and every decision we make should be aligned with our core values or we end up in conflict, and disappointed, with ourselves.

Core values show up in all aspects of our lives. Sometimes our values are challenged during periods of high stress and change when it is more important than ever to know exactly what they are. If we consistently follow our core values, decisions are easier. We no longer vacillate between right and wrong; we automatically know the correct choice for us.

Do You Know Your "Why?"

Rob once had the pleasure of coaching and employing a thirty-one-year-old man named Nick, a hard worker who knows his core values and his "why." Nick started working for Rob in a 9:00–5:00 job that conflicted with his core values of sleeping in and enjoying free time and independence. After ninety days, with Rob's support, Nick quit his job because he was unhappy with his schedule. Today, Nick enjoys a flexible profession that allows him to walk dogs in his free time, pursue his hobbies, wake up and go to bed when he chooses, and exercise on his own schedule. It is important to him to have that freedom and day-to-day balance.

Do you want to live a life of integrity in which your actions align with your personal values and beliefs? You might be struggling to make a big decision or find direction in your life. Your core values are the needle of your compass that allows you to be true to yourself. In the following exercise, get clear with your values and uncover your true identity and passions.

● TBE EXERCISE

Core Values

Situations that allow you to be authentic, genuine, and real are probably aligned with your core values. Below is a list of sample core values. If some of your core values are missing from this list, add them. Think about how you feel about each value, then circle the five that are most important to you. The goal is to end up with your top five core values.

- **Adventure**—Are you willing to try new things?
- **Attitude**—Do you approach the day and the world with a positive attitude?
- **Career**—Is the work you do a priority in your life?
- **Courage**—Do you face difficulties head on?
- **Empathy**—Do you think about and understand other people's feelings and perspectives?
- **Faith**—Do you have trust or confidence in someone or something?
- **Fun**—Do you incorporate fun into your day? See chapter eight for the importance of fun.
- **Gratitude**—Do you spend time thinking about what and whom you are grateful for?
- **Happiness**—Do you make happiness a priority? Do you do things that make you happy?
- **Health**—Is being healthy in your mind, body, and spirit important to you?
- **Honesty**—Are you open and honest with people in your life?

- **Humor**—Do you laugh often, including at yourself?
- **Humility**—Do you listen to and accept others without taking power and control?
- **Independence**—Do you have control over your life?
- **Integrity**—Do you have a clear idea of what you believe is right and wrong?
- **Kindness**—Do you have concern for others without any expectations?
- **Knowledge**—Is learning new things and acquiring new skills important to you?
- **Mindfulness**—Are you conscious of your feelings, thoughts, and emotions?
- **Respect**—Do you treat others the way you want to be treated?
- **Safety**—Is your environment safe? Are your relationships safe? Do you feel safe?
- **Service**—Do you embrace opportunities to contribute to the common good?
- **Social**—Is interacting with other people important to you?
- **Success**—Are you achieving your objectives and goals?
- **Wealth**—Is financial independence important to you?
- **Wisdom**—Are you accumulating life experiences and knowledge?

Let's look more closely at an example. If you circled Independence, you value being able to create your ideal schedule each day. You might value the freedom to work from home or anywhere in the world. Focusing on independence as a top core value allows you to create it in your life. Here are some examples of actions—some are Micro-moves™ and some are major shifts—you could take to more fully align your life with your core value of independence. You could:

- Find a career or job that would allow you more freedom during the day
- Build a life that allows you to create your own schedule, travel, try new things, etc.
- Nurture relationships with friends and family who give you the freedom to be yourself
- Become your own boss
- Include significant free time in your schedule

The point of the values list is that you number them from one to five and then live your life accordingly. Are you living a life of prayer? Do you have integrity? Are you involved in community or service? The values exercise is designed to help you be aware of and live according to your top five values. Feel free to add to the list.

Now let's move on to the second aspect of self, personal time.

Personal Time

Self = Core Values + **Personal Time** + Development + Work + Spiritual

Do you have enough personal time in your life? This is *your* time, the time to do anything you choose.

Many of us are not good at spending time alone and feel guilty when we do. We are conditioned through school and work to believe that continuous productivity is important. However, research shows that productivity declines after ninety minutes of deep focus. The same research reveals that we are lucky to have two deep focus periods per day. The point is, personal time helps us recharge, regroup, and reflect. If you don't make time for yourself, you start resenting your life and everything you do. Because it's so important to spend time being with ourselves, personal time should be scheduled like everything else. Your personal time might include the following activities:

- Lying on the couch and watching TV
- Taking a coffee break
- Journaling
- Taking a walk
- Enjoying nature
- People watching
- Thinking
- Doing nothing
- Reading
- Moseying, strolling, or sauntering about
- Listening to music

How much time should you schedule to be alone with yourself? While we don't recommend scheduling every single minute of the day, your priorities should be scheduled with the same level of importance as a work meeting or doctor's appointment. Self should be a priority—there should be a block in your day for personal time to do whatever you want.

Please note that time for self does not include sleeping, though it certainly could include lying in bed thinking, meditating, reading, or journaling.

Making time to be alone with ourselves should be a primary focus. Research shows that this alone time is important for both personal and professional growth.

You should also allow for time each day without screens. While you can spend endless amounts of time on your computer or phone, it's important to manage your screen time before it gets out of control and begins to manage you. Sometimes we need to take a break from all the news and craziness in the world, so make sure you plan for downtime from screens.

Jeff Bezos, one of the wealthiest people in the world, uses the time slot of 8:00 a.m.–10:00 a.m. for what he calls "puttering" (we call it "moseying"). This is his time to do as he chooses. Every morning he wakes up, drinks his coffee while reading the newspaper, and has breakfast with his kids before his work schedule takes over. Work has a definite time slot from 10:00 a.m.–5:00 p.m. every day, but personal time has its time slots as well.

Now let's turn to the third component of self, development.

Development—Personal and Professional

Self = Core Values + Personal Time + **Development** + Work + Spiritual

The world is changing rapidly as we accommodate ever more apps, video streaming, online courses, and anywhere, anytime education. We have abundant opportunities to develop ourselves, both personally and professionally, whenever it is most convenient for us. For example, thanks to YouTube, we can learn just about anything in a few minutes. We live in a world that values skills. The more we have, the more valuable we are to ourselves and to others.

The key is to avoid becoming overwhelmed. Instead of lamenting that you'll never finish that three-hundred-page book, make the Micro-move™

of reading a few pages at a time. You do not have to learn it all or do it all at once, but learning helps us feel good about ourselves. If you learn one new thing a week, after fifty-two weeks, you'll have learned fifty-two new things. Read one book a month and that's twelve books in a year, 120 books in ten years. The numbers add up, but this isn't about the numbers. Rather, it's about your personal and professional learning and growth. Many employers will reimburse or pay for personal/professional development, and that makes learning feel even better. In other words, you can get paid to grow!

🏃 TBE IN ACTION

A Novel Kind of Development

A few years ago, Rob and his boss/partner Marc, CEO of STS education, visited Blackwell's Book Shoppe, established in 1879, while traveling through the UK. They saw sixteen books wrapped in plain brown paper, each with a brief summary but no author or title. This section of the store was titled, "You can't judge a book by its cover."

Marc decided to create a book club to encourage company employees to read. Today, the STS Education team receives an incentive to read by getting paid $25, $50, or $100 based upon the length of the book and by submitting a one-page review on how the book helps them grow personally, in their job, and in the company as a whole. Books can include any one of a selection of wrapped books that are continuously replenished and contain a brief statement about the book without revealing the title or author.

To date, the employees have read and reviewed more than 1,200 books with more than $40,000 paid out for their personal development. A by-product of this initiative is that employees are comfortable making recommendations. And, yes, there's a substantial correlation between how many books are read and personal and company growth: the company has grown more than one hundred percent in the past two years.

One employee, a young man in an entry-level position, leapfrogged to the very important position of Salesforce administrator within a year of becoming active in the book club. Marc, the CEO, supported David in learning the skills to assume the position. Within another year, David left the company earning more than double what he'd earned as a technology supervisor. What allowed David to rise so quickly? His book reports, which helped Marc realize how capable he was.

Work

Self = Core Values + Personal Time + Development + **Work** + Spiritual

The fourth component of self is work. Do you enjoy your work? We hope so because you probably spend as much, if not more, time working as you do sleeping. You should feel good about the work you do and excited to get up and go to work, whether remotely or to another location.

In *Getting Things Done—The Art of Stress-Free Productivity*, author David Allen talks about having a more peaceful workday routine while still thriving, being more productive, and managing time without stress. While that might be easier said than done, work helps define how we feel about ourselves both positively and negatively. We need to do our best not to settle for something less than we deserve.

Making time for breaks during the workday increases productivity, as does vacation time. Stephen Covey, the author of *7 Habits of Highly Effective People*, felt so strongly about getting away from the daily routine to vacation at least a few times a year that he created a habit called "sharpening the saw." He saw this habit as critical for maximizing effectiveness at work. Covey says that as soon as you get back to work, you should plan for your next vacation and put it on your calendar so you can look forward to it.

Work hard but make time to disconnect and recharge so that you can be optimally effective on an ongoing basis. Setting boundaries between work and personal life allows for harmony. People who feel good about work are more likely to feel good about themselves, which carries over into all the other categories of the Balance Equation™. When we blur the boundaries between personal and professional values, we might think we are getting more done, but in reality, we are less effective in both areas. With that fact in mind, take a moment to engage in the exercise below, which will clarify how you feel about work.

 TBE EXERCISE

How Do You Feel about Work?

Answer the three questions below with a simple "yes" or "no." No equivocating allowed.

- Do you like what you do?
- Do you like who you do it with and for?
- Do you feel good about the value (time, money, passion, etc.) you receive for your job?

If you can answer "yes" to these three questions, congratulations! You likely feel good about your work. If you responded "no" to one or more questions, you might want to make time to think about what it will take to get to "yes" in all three areas.

Spiritual

Self = Core Values + Personal Time + Development + Work + **Spiritual**

The fifth component of self is spiritual. Spirituality is different for all of us. Some individuals are more spiritual than others, and that's okay. Perhaps you aren't spiritual at all but have a special place or two where you feel your best, such as the ocean, the mountains, or in your home. Place is also part of spirituality for many of us. You may be part of a congregation or believe in a higher power or source but prefer not to attend organized group gatherings. Regardless, making time for meditation, reflection, visualization, affirmation, reading, journaling, or any other activity you consider to be spiritual will be rewarding. The key is to make time for what is important to you. Once again, this is the power of the Balance Equation™. If spirituality is important to you, make time for it.

Psychiatrist Viktor Frankl's memoir, *Man's Search for Meaning*, has riveted generations of readers with its descriptions of life in a Nazi death camp and its lessons for spiritual survival. Based on his own experience and the stories of his patients, Frankl argues that we cannot avoid suffering but we can choose how to cope with it, find meaning in it, and move forward with renewed purpose. At the heart of his theory, known as logotherapy, is the conviction that the primary human drive is not pleasure but the pursuit of what we find meaningful. *Man's Search for Meaning* has become one of the most influential books in America. It continues to inspire us all to find significance in the very act of living.

The Importance of Place in Our Lives

The expression "Home is where the heart is" highlights the importance of place and places in our lives. This statement includes where we live, where we work, where we eat, where we hike, where we exercise, where we worship, where we laugh, where we cheer, where we grieve, where we cry, where we love and are loved—in short, where we do most of the important things in our lives.

Many wars are based on one side invading another's homeland with the intent of taking it from them. The ongoing Russia/Ukraine War is an example of this type of conflict. Russia invaded Ukraine and the Ukrainians fought back to protect and hold on to their country—their place.

Place includes the importance and core value of security and feeling secure, which is one of the needs identified in Abraham Maslow's celebrated hierarchy of needs displayed in the chart on the next page. Safety, at the second level, becomes very important after physiological needs (food, water, and clothing) are met. No matter where you are in the world, you will almost always have an emotional connection to the place you call home. People are willing to pay more or less, accept or reject a job offer, and leave or stay with family and friends to live where they choose. The importance of place includes many of the core values mentioned earlier in the chapter and plays an important role in helping us all achieve balance in our lives.

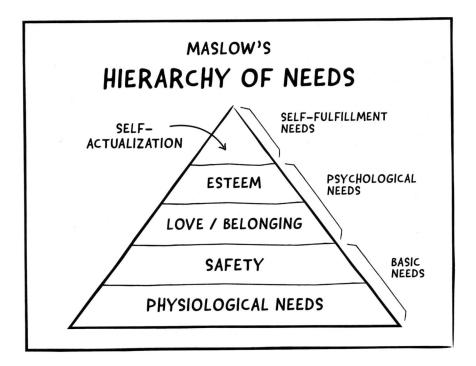

🌑 TBE EXERCISE

Assess Your Self

Take the TBE assessment below. For the moment, ignore the QR code. Ponder the smiley faces and circle how you feel:

SELF

Core Values	1	2	3	4	5
Personal	1	2	3	4	5
Development	1	2	3	4	5
Work	1	2	3	4	5
Spirituality	1	2	3	4	5

Add up your numbers from each subcategory and record this total number below.

Total Self: _____

This number reflects how you currently feel about yourself. Now, choose your *lowest* number from the subcategories above, circle it, and begin one Micro-move™ from each category listed below. Feel free to add one or more of your own if you are so inspired.

✍ SELF MICRO-MOVES™

Core Values
- If kindness is one of your core values, say good morning to everyone.
- If learning is one of your core values, learn something new every day.
- If family is one of your core values, spend time with them today.

Personal

- Add two minutes to your normal shower.
- Add a minute to breathe and focus on your breath.
- Subtract a to-do-list item that is not urgent or important.

Development

- Read one page in a book or listen to a podcast for a few minutes.
- Identify a skill you want to develop.
- Join a new group like LinkedIn or your local chamber of commerce.

Work

- Learn a new computer skill.
- Reach out to a colleague you don't know.
- Take a walk during your break.

Spirituality

- Meditate for a few minutes.
- List three things you are grateful for.
- Spend time in prayer.

RECAP

Self = Core Values + Personal + Development + Work + Spiritual

If you don't feel good about yourself, then all the other major categories (health, relationships, and money) are affected. When you want to make a change in your life, once you truly know what is important to you, make a Micro-move™ to begin that change. Eliminate autopilot by staying conscious about how you feel. How you spend your time should reflect your priorities. Remember:

- Self-care is essential.
- All your behaviors and decisions should be aligned with your core values.
- Personal time is time to do anything you choose and should be scheduled like everything else.
- The more skills you develop, the more valuable you are to yourself and others.
- If you feel good about work, you are more likely to feel good about yourself.
- If spirituality is important to you, then make time for it. If it isn't, then don't.
- Keep in mind that your past does not define your future.

Now that you have an understanding of self, one of the four major categories of the Balance Equation™, let's move on to the next chapter and explore your health.

A Deep Dive into Health

The Balance Equation™ = Self + **Health** + Relationships + Money

You need to be proactive, carve out time in your schedule, and take responsibility for being the healthiest person you can be—no one else is going to do it for you.

—Dr. Mehmet Oz

Health is one of the four main categories of the Balance Equation™. If you don't feel good about your health, then all the other categories (self, relationships, and money) are affected.

Health = Physical + Mental + Social Emotional + Food + Sleep

According to the World Health Organization, health is a state of complete physical, mental, and social well-being, not merely the absence of disease or infirmity. How do you feel about your health? Look at the five smiley faces below and answer the question.

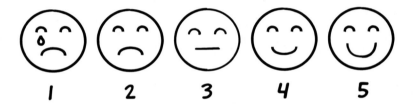

Let's also take a closer look at the five subcategories of health, which add up to how you feel about your current well-being. It takes time, effort, and consistency to maintain good health, and it should be a priority if you want to be healthy.

Think about a time you've been sick when you had to stop what you were doing to care for yourself. That period of time must be subtracted from the time you could be doing other things. And keep in mind that ignoring symptoms can lead to a more serious illness with more time taken away from other priorities, which is why we feel out of balance when we are sick.

How you feel about your health is determined by your level of consciousness about how you're doing in all aspects of this category. A self-check-in where you assess your feelings about the current state of your physical, mental, social-emotional, nutritional, and sleep patterns is important, so let's dive into the five subcategories of health.

Physical

Health = **Physical +** Mental + Social Emotional + Food + Sleep

Physical health represents one dimension of our total well-being. The term refers to the state of our physical body and how well it operates. If you struggle with your physical health, you might want to take a look at Project School Wellness, which offers lesson plans for skills-based health educators who want to change students' lives. These ready-to-teach lesson plans align with National Health Education Standards, are comprehensive, and allow in-person or digital learning. You can find all sorts of resources for improving your physical health.

It's important to take into account the condition of your body by considering everything from the absence of disease to your fitness level. Take a moment to ask yourself the following questions:

- How do I feel physically?
- Do I exercise regularly and maintain healthy habits that support my physical well-being?
- Am I moving throughout the day?
- Do I spend time outdoors?
- Do I have any unhealthy habits that affect my physical health?

Our physical health is strongly connected to all the other subcategories (mental, emotional, nutrition, and sleep) within the greater health category. If you've taken the assessment, you know how you feel about your physical health and can prioritize what you want to work on to feel better. You might want to lose weight, but is that a priority in your life? What jumps out at you as something you'd like to work on? It only takes a few minutes to check in with how you feel about your health.

Find What Works for You

Even though physical health is something a lot of people struggle with, we all need to practice self-compassion and be proud of maintaining a physically healthy lifestyle—it helps in ways few of us realize. If you struggle to fit time into your busy schedule to take care of yourself physically, that is totally understandable, but you can use Micro-moves™ to make small changes that will add up to big results. A good example of a morning Micro-move™ is a one-minute stretch before you get out of bed.

Another Micro-move™ might be starting a fitness journal. All you need is a notebook, an Excel spreadsheet on your computer, or your phone, and it's also a good idea to plan ahead what muscle groups you're going to work on before heading to the gym. A clear plan will help maximize your results and take the guesswork out of what you're going to do when you get there, while keeping a journal will help you exercise with an objective and purpose.

☞ MAKE A HEALTH MICRO-MOVE™ TODAY

Do some type of exercise today. What will you do? Go for a walk? Take a fitness class? Lift weights at home? As the famous Nike slogan says, "Just do it."

Mental

Health = Physical **+ Mental** + Social Emotional + Food + Sleep

Mental health includes our emotional, psychological, and social well-being. It affects how we think, feel, and act and helps determine how we handle stress, relate to others, recover from difficulties and setbacks, and make choices. Being mentally or emotionally healthy means more than being free of depression, anxiety, or other psychiatric illnesses. Mental health is important at every stage of life, from childhood and adolescence through adulthood.

Over the course of your life, if you experience mental health problems, your thought processes, mood, and behavior could be affected. Many factors contribute to mental health problems, including:

- Biological factors such as genes or brain chemistry
- Life experiences such as trauma or abuse
- A family history of mental health problems

According to the World Health Organization, mental health is a "state of well-being in which an individual realizes his or her own abilities, can cope with the normal stresses of life, can work productively, and is able to make a contribution to his or her community." When we refer to mental health, we are talking about psychological and emotional well-being.

Mental health problems can be temporary or permanent, but many people overcome mental health issues. Look at the chart below and assess how you feel about your mental health at this moment.

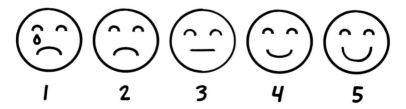

Ask yourself:

- Do I enjoy life and laugh and have fun?
- Am I able to deal with stress and bounce back from adversity?
- Do I feel a sense of meaning and purpose in both my activities and relationships?
- Am I flexible and adaptable to change?
- Am I able to build and maintain fulfilling relationships?

Movement of any kind helps strengthen us mentally as well as physically. Taking a morning walk to the ocean or nearby natural area, performing pushups while the tea steeps, or taking a break from the computer to do some stretching are all Micro-moves™ that make you feel better.

Check Your Lifestyle—Does It Support Your Mental Health?

It's helpful to recognize the ways your lifestyle could be unintentionally hindering your ability to manage your emotions and cope with hardship. For example, what does your support system look like? Having someone you can talk to, whether it's a friend, family member, coach, teacher, or coworker, is remarkably helpful in maintaining mental health. It's imperative to be able to express how we feel to the people in our lives. Zoom and Skype are great ways to connect with people who are far away.

Consider Meditation

Meditation is a great way to regulate and become aware of our emotions. We are currently living in a 24/7 world of news: real news, fake news, and a continuous flow of all forms of media. COVID-19 death rates include the young, the old, and the middle aged. Enough already! Unfortunately, bad news seems to overshadow any positive headlines. This makes it very difficult to find inner peace, but meditation can help us throughout the day.

Most studies highlight the strong benefits of ten to twelve minutes of meditation per day. In fact, research shows it's as important for your brain as cardio is for your heart.

● TBE EXERCISE

Make Meditation a Micro-move™

Find a quiet place to meditate as part of your morning routine. In addition, meditate whenever you feel stressed or have too much anxiety, meditate before bed, and meditate when you feel extra stressed. All you have to do is sit quietly, close your eyes, and focus on your breath. Start with one minute and build from there. Meditating is also a great way to practice a self-check-in to see how you are feeling. Notice where you feel your breath in your body.

It's Okay to Not Be Okay

In an article posted in the *Harvard Business Review* titled "It's Okay to Not Be Okay," Dr. Jaime Zuckerman points out how important it is to allow yourself to not feel okay, to accept the thoughts, feelings, and sensations you are experiencing, and to sit with them until they pass. If you try to suppress or ignore your feelings, they often grow stronger, leaving you feeling overwhelmed and unable to cope. The good news is that no emotion is permanent. We all know that happiness, joy, anger, frustration, and sadness come and go. We have experienced similar feelings throughout our lives and have learned that it's okay not to be okay. Today, we allow ourselves to feel the feelings and know it is a sign of strength to ask for help.

Ask for Help

Talking to a mental health expert is not only fine but often is vitally important. It's okay to ask for and get help. There are many examples of courageous people who have stopped in their tracks, paid attention to their feelings and emotions, put their mental health first, and asked for help. One recent example is *Time* magazine's 2021 Athlete of the Year, Simone Biles, who exemplified this type of courage during the 2021 Olympic games when she withdrew from the gymnastics competition to take care of her mental health.

Practice Resilience

Like Kobe Bryant, we all experience disappointment, loss, and change. While these experiences are a normal part of life, they still cause sadness, anxiety, and stress. Physically healthy people are better able to bounce back from illness or injury, and people with strong mental health are better able to bounce back from adversity, trauma, and stress. This skill is called resilience. People who are emotionally and mentally resilient have the tools to cope with difficult situations while maintaining a positive outlook. How do you build resilience? Try the items on the list below:

- Practice self-compassion.
- Maintain a positive outlook on the future.
- Be empathetic.
- Learn to relax.
- Think before reacting.
- Set attainable goals.
- Develop strong relationships.
- Learn from your mistakes.
- Be flexible/adaptable.

- Practice self-compassion.
- When you get to the bottom of the list, rinse and repeat.

Social Emotional

Health = Physical + Mental + **Social Emotional** + Food + Sleep

Our social-emotional health is intrinsically connected to the other health subcategories, specifically mental health. Not surprisingly, relationships are a giant part of our social emotional health.

Relationships

We'll take a closer look at relationships in the next chapter, but for now, we simply want to share that the Harvard Happiness Study, which started in 1938 during the Great Depression, found a strong association between happiness and close relationships, whether with spouses, family members, friends, or social circles. In short, personal connection creates mental and emotional stimulation that automatically boosts moods, while isolating yourself is a mood buster. This ongoing study, one of the world's longest studies of adult life, reveals that those who fare the best are those who lean into relationships with family, friends, and their community.

Tellingly, research completed on patients with congestive heart failure has shown that satisfactory relationships can significantly improve physical health. Over a four-year period, those in happier relationships were less likely to die compared to those in unhappier relationships, as shown in the chart on the next page. Other studies have shown that the quality of our relationships indicates more about a person's overall subjective well-being than does their satisfaction with any other domain of life, including work, finances, community, and health.

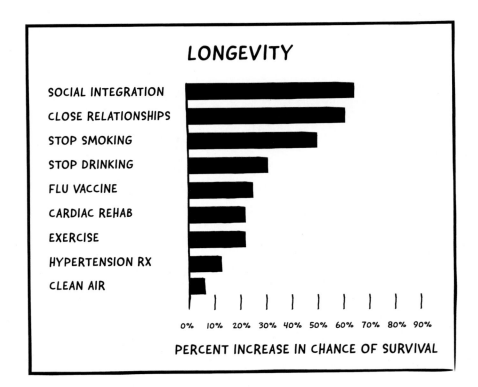

LONGEVITY

SOCIAL INTEGRATION
CLOSE RELATIONSHIPS
STOP SMOKING
STOP DRINKING
FLU VACCINE
CARDIAC REHAB
EXERCISE
HYPERTENSION RX
CLEAN AIR

0% 10% 20% 30% 40% 50% 60% 70% 80% 90%

PERCENT INCREASE IN CHANCE OF SURVIVAL

Life Skills

Being healthy socially and emotionally requires being able to understand, experience, express, and manage emotions and develop meaningful relationships with others. Ask yourself:

- Am I satisfied with the current state of my emotional skills?
- Do I have strong, fulfilling social relationships?
- Is my well-being improving?

We must be able to manage our own emotions and understand how our personal life experiences impact us to feel compassion, empathy, love, and gratitude and to develop critical life skills.

We've all attended those dreaded social events at which we need to interact with people we've never met. It's not easy to get past our fears of interacting with strangers. Having the skills to introduce yourself and begin conversing with people you don't know is a social norm that allows you to break the ice and gain momentum in your interactions. Saying "Hello," "Good morning," "Good evening," "Please," and "Thank you" are all Micro-moves™ that set the tone for positive interactions. These skills apply to all forms of communications such as email, text, and phone.

Self-awareness and self-management are necessary skills that develop and strengthen our social awareness and relationship skills. These four aspects of social-emotional wellness contribute to our ability to make responsible decisions and also to bring our core values into our daily lives.

Social awareness is a person's ability to consider the perspectives of other individuals, groups, or communities and apply that understanding to interactions with them. We continue to develop these skills throughout our lives as we encounter new and different relationships that allow us to understand other people's points of view.

Personal awareness allows us to be conscious of our social interactions, which enables us to function in society. This means developing the skills necessary to empathize and relate to others from diverse backgrounds. We acquire these skills from different sources such family, friends, school, work, teams, community groups, and other life interactions.

Listening

Listening is an extremely important skill that can have a major impact on our relationships as well as our effectiveness at work. According to Edgar Dale, the author of *Cone of Experience*, we only remember twenty-five to fifty percent of what we hear. Therefore, listening is a skill we can all improve. By becoming active listeners, we can influence, negotiate, persuade, and improve our productivity. This also helps us avoid misunderstandings and conflicts. Practicing active listening means making a conscious effort to be present and focused on what the other person is saying. An easy Micro-move™ is to put away your phone and eliminate any other multi-tasking that distracts you.

Food

Health = Physical + Mental + Social Emotional + **Food** + Sleep

The fourth component of health is food, which means maintaining a balanced diet that includes the recommended nutrients, food groups, and calories for your age and height, consuming the recommended amount of water daily, and taking the proper vitamins and supplements for your needs. Ask yourself:

- How do I feel about food?
- Do I eat a healthy, balanced diet?
- Do I drink the recommended amount of water daily?
- Do I take necessary vitamins and supplements?

If you value a healthy mind and body, you know how important it is to have a balanced diet. Our intake of food, water, other fluids, and vitamins is the fuel that keeps us functioning well throughout the day, and it all starts with drinking enough water. Adult men are made up of about sixty percent water, adult women about fifty percent. We need to continually replenish this water for our bodies to operate efficiently. Do you know how many ounces of water you drink per day? According to the American

Medical Association, we're all supposed to drink at least eight glasses of water, or sixty-four ounces, per day. Studies show that more than half the population is dehydrated because people drink caffeinated and other beverages that act as diuretics and dry them out, thus requiring them to drink even more water. Eating well and avoiding junk food is something a lot of people struggle with. It's often hard to recognize the benefits of a healthy diet, particularly if you've never experienced them. Food isn't always part of the school curriculum, and many parents don't know how to properly feed their children. Knowledge isn't the only component of why we choose our diet. There is comfort in routine and with the foods we grew up eating, and eating itself is often a mindless activity. Take this moment to practice some self-compassion and write down everything you eat in a day. You might be surprised by what you find. Just do it for one day and then ask yourself the following questions:

- How do I feel about my list?
- Am I surprised?
- Are there areas where I could make healthier choices?
- Do I need to drink more water?
- Do I eat to fuel my body or for other reasons?

⫸🏃 TBE IN ACTION

Diedre's Journey to Better Health
We have known Diedre for years. A great person and excellent massage therapist, she's been on a journey to better health for many years. After losing her dad at the age of twenty-five, she was on a downward spiral before finally coming out

of depression. One of the things that helped her most was the Buddhist chant she and her husband voice in the mornings and evenings, "Nam nyoho renge kyo," which is a pledge to never yield to difficulties and to triumph over suffering.

Chanting helped change Diedre's outlook and enabled her to see things in a different light. She believes it rewired her brain so that she could embrace happiness from within.

She also found ways to make it easier to eat a healthy diet without following any specific eating plan other than focusing on healthy, wholesome meals. She has followed the practice of weekly meal preparation to help her eat healthier meals and continues to lose weight, feel good, and overall live a healthier lifestyle. The picture below shows Diedre's meal preparation in action.

DIEDRE'S WEEKLY MEAL PREP

To date, using Micro-moves™ to lose weight in small incre-
ments that target an even number, Diedre has lost more than
140 pounds. Most of all, she is consistent. If she falls off the
wagon one day, so to speak, she gets right back to eating well
the next meal or next day. Practicing the chant, even for one
minute a day, changes her energy in a good way, helps her help
herself, and propels her forward to a happier, healthier life.

Listen to Your Body

Be conscious of the food choices you make and how they affect your body.
For example, caffeine affects some of us more than others. In fact, studies
show that for each cup of caffeine we consume, we should drink one glass
of water.

In addition to what we eat, *when* we eat snacks and meals factors into
our overall health. Studies show that eating dinner late and snacking before
retiring affect our sleep patterns. Researchers recommend that we stop all
eating and drinking three or more hours before going to bed for optimal
sleep. A Micro-move™ would be to stop eating thirty minutes earlier than
your normal routine. Another Micro-move™ would be to drink a glass of
water when you wake up each morning.

Sleep

Health = Physical **+** Mental + Social Emotional + Food + **Sleep**

The final component of health is sleep. According to Christopher Barnes
at *Harvard Business Review*, "Although experts recommend eight hours of
sleep a night, many of us don't get that. A recent study of leaders across the
world found that forty-two percent, on average, get six hours of shuteye or
less." Insufficient rest is a huge problem that leads to poor judgment, lack of

self-control, and impaired creativity. The chart below from the National Sleep Foundation highlights how much sleep each of us should get for our age.

Fortunately, there are ways to get more and better rest. They include sticking to a regular bedtime and wake-up time; avoiding caffeine, nicotine, alcohol, and screen time before bed; tracking your sleep patterns and adjusting accordingly, such as getting treatment for sleep disorders; and napping during the workday. If you make sleep a priority, you'll probably be more productive.

The CDC recommends that healthy adults get at least six to eight hours of sleep per night, which, on average, is about one-third of our lives. Sleep is necessary for our bodies to rest, repair, and recover. Depending on our circumstances, we all need different amounts of sleep. A quick part of your self-check-in should be assessing your sleep as soon as you wake up.

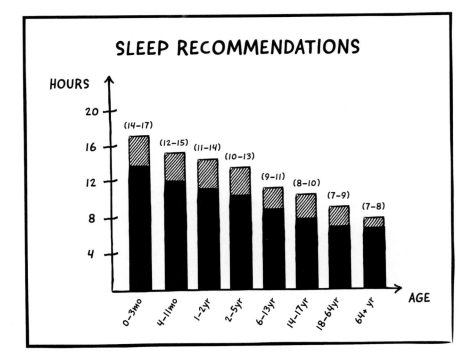

Ask yourself, "How do I feel when I wake up each morning?" The answer could be different every day.

Sleep is such an integral part of our overall health that it can impact the other subcategories (physical, mental, social emotional, and nutrition). Sleeping well gives us the energy to maintain good physical health. Good sleep is also linked to improved concentration, productivity, and overall mood. It also affects our appetites and what we choose to eat. To become a better sleeper, sleep needs to be a priority. This means that sleep, like everything else that's important to us, needs to be scheduled.

⊒🏃 TBE IN ACTION

Sherry's Sleep Routine

Our friend Sherry is adamant about sticking to her sleep schedule. Going to bed at approximately the same time every night ensures she gets at least nine hours of shuteye. About an hour before bed, she takes 500 mg of calcium with 250 mg of magnesium—the combination works well to lower blood pressure and ensure a good night's sleep. After taking a shower and washing her face, she uses her favorite facial moisturizer, moisturizes her feet with lavender and chamomile lotion, and climbs into bed to read a good book. When she can't read another word, she shuts off the light and is asleep in five minutes. Sticking to her sleep schedule ensures that she gets plenty of rest and wakes up refreshed and ready to face the day. Below are several sleep-related Micro-moves™ that can improve your Balance Equation™ in this category too.

SLEEP MICRO-MOVES™

1. Schedule your day around a consistent time you want to go to sleep and wake up.
2. Stop all eating and drinking two to three hours before bedtime.
3. Keep your bedroom as cold as possible.
4. Keep your room as dark as possible.
5. Sign off from all screens (phone, computer, TV, etc.) an hour before bed.
6. Keep your phone out of the bedroom.
7. Invest in a comfortable bed.
8. Invest in a comfortable pillow.
9. Dress comfortably.
10. Reduce or eliminate your caffeine, nicotine, and alcohol intake.

Now that you've learned about health and the five subcategories of physical, mental, social emotional, nutrition, and sleep, think about how you feel. Revisit the chart below and assign a number between one and five to each subcategory. Has anything changed? Has it changed for the better or worse? Is there anything you can or want to do about that?

TBE EXERCISE

Assess Your Health

How do you feel about your health at this point in time? For the moment, ignore the QR code. Instead, look at the five smiley faces below and circle how you feel in each of the five subcategories.

| 1 | 2 | 3 | 4 | 5 |

HEALTH

Physical	1	2	3	4	5
Mental	1	2	3	4	5
Social Emotional	1	2	3	4	5
Food	1	2	3	4	5
Sleep	1	2	3	4	5

Add your number from each subcategory and record it below.

Total Health: _____

This total health number above is how you currently feel about your health category. Now choose the lowest number from the subcategories above, then circle and begin one Micro-move™ from the list below. As before, feel free to add one or more of your own Micro-moves™ if you're so inspired.

☝ HEALTH MICRO-MOVES™

Physical
- Schedule time to exercise today for five to ten minutes.
- Take a break from your work and go for a walk.
- Use the stairs instead of the elevator.

Mental
- Take a few minutes to meditate.
- Put your favorite music on while you work.
- Practice deep breathing for a minute when you get anxious or stressed.

Social Emotional
- Send a thank-you text to a coworker for a job well done.
- Practice your listening skills during a Zoom meeting.
- Tell a family member or friend that you love or appreciate them.

Food
- Drink a glass of water when you wake up.
- Start your dinner 30 minutes earlier.
- Keep a healthy snack like an apple or banana on hand at all times.

Sleep

- Turn off your devices before bed.
- Drink a cup of chamomile tea before bed.
- Reduce room temperature by a few degrees.

RECAP

Health = Physical + Mental + Social Emotional + Food + Sleep

If you don't feel good about your health, then all the other major categories (self, relationships, and money) are affected. When you want to make a change in your life, once you truly know what is important for you, make a Micro-move™ to begin that change. Eliminate autopilot by staying conscious about how you feel. How you spend your time should reflect your priorities. Remember:

- Health is a state of complete physical, mental, and social well-being and not merely the absence of disease or infirmity.
- It takes time, effort, and consistency to maintain good health, and it should be a priority if you want to be healthy.
- It's important to assess how you feel about the condition of your body by doing a self-check-in daily; this Micro-move™ only takes one minute of your time.
- Always remember to practice self-compassion and applaud your efforts.
- Meditation is a great way to regulate and become aware of your emotions.
- It's okay to ask for help.

- Social-emotional health includes the capacity to understand, experience, express, and manage emotions and to develop meaningful relationships with others.
- We can all improve our self-awareness, self-management, and listening skills.
- In addition to the choices we make nutritionally, the timing of when we eat is also very important.
- Schedule your day around a consistent time you want to go to sleep and wake up, and embrace habits that encourage good sleep.

Now that you have an understanding of health, one of the four major categories of the Balance Equation™, let's move on to the next chapter and explore relationships in greater detail.

A Deep Dive into Relationships

The Balance Equation™ = Self + Health + **Relationships** + Money

I've learned that people will forget what you said.
People will forget what you did, but people will
never forget how you made them feel.

—Maya Angelou

The Balance Equation™ = Self + Health + **Relationships** + Money

Relationships are one of the four main categories of the Balance Equation™. If you don't feel good about your relationships, then all the other categories (self, health, and money) are affected.

Relationships = Most Significant + Family + Friends + Work + Inner Circle

Relationships are the way people feel and behave towards each other. This includes the connections we make with people we interact with throughout our lives. Healthy relationships share key characteristics such as trust, respect, affection, and openness.

Together, the five relationship subcategories add up to how we feel about the people in our lives. How do you feel about *your* relationships? Look at the five smiley faces below and answer the question.

Relationships are so important that our brains are hardwired to form them. In the movie *Castaway,* Tom Hanks' character, stranded on an uninhabited island, creates a face on a volleyball, names it "Wilson," and talks to it as if it were a person. Though fictional and funny, the gesture illustrates a very basic human need.

Relationships are enormously important for health, and there are many studies on the biological processes that account for the link between relationships and health. For one thing, relationships can help reduce stress, which in turn reduces our cortisol levels and puts less stress on our adrenal glands, but relationships do take constant nurturing. It takes time, effort, and consistency to maintain them, and doing so should be a priority.

The Harvard Medical School study cited earlier that first studied men and then added women highlighted how relationships make a big difference in individual levels of happiness for the "happy well" and "happy unwell" groups. While the study mentioned seven big areas that can affect long-term happiness as we age, the single most impactful area is healthy relationships in marriage and with friends and partners. An inspiring quote from Robert Waldinger, who currently directs the study, is this: "Well-being can be built, and the best building blocks are good, warm relationships."

Healthy Relationships Take Constant Nurturing

Healthy relationships can be nurtured with small gestures of kindness. Once again, this is where Micro-moves™ can be helpful. Conveying to someone that you love them through a note, text, or short call are all examples of Micro-moves™.

Why is it that so many of us put off these tiny gestures for a later time? Often, it is because we think bigger, more time-consuming macro-moves are needed such as arranging for flowers or gifts, texting later when we can compose a masterpiece, or calling later when we have a full half hour to talk. On the contrary, it's better not to wait but to reach out with small gestures now.

Do Not Wait—Do It Now

Many of us talk ourselves into perfection, which often leads to procrastination that results in missed opportunities to express our true thoughts and feelings towards someone we care about. Good relationships take nurturing, and Micro-moves™ are enough most of the time—and the more frequent, the better.

It's a sad fact that many of us lose loved ones earlier than expected. In the COVID-19 world, someone can get the virus and end up dying alone, unable to tell their loved ones they love them, and vice versa. Do not miss an opportunity to nurture your relationships. Make a Micro-move™. Consider one from the list below or add your own.

☞ RELATIONSHIP MICRO-MOVES™

- Plan a date night with your spouse or significant other.
- Send an "I'm thinking of you" text.
- Leave post-it notes for your spouse, family member, or friend.
- Tell someone at work, "You're doing a great job."
- Say "Hello" or "Good morning" to someone at work, your barista, or even a stranger.
- Send a picture or link to make a connection.

Good relationships take time, but not necessarily a lot of time. The most significant people in your life deserve to be a priority. They are usually top of mind, so let them know this.

How do you create time for the most significant people in your life? Like everything else, you schedule it. That means blocking time on your calendar. With this simple task on the table, let's dive into the five subcategories of relationships.

Most Significant

Relationships = **Most Significant** + Family +Friends + Work + Inner Circle

Most of us do not take the time to think about and identify the most significant person in our lives. The most significant person in your life is exactly that: the person you consider to be your highest priority no matter what. This could be your partner, child, parent, friend, or pet. Your most significant other is typically someone you have a mutual connection and understanding with. Typically, you are each other's most significant other.

Who is *your* most significant other? Take the time to think about this question. If you don't currently have a most significant, that's okay. Significant relationships change and evolve over time. If you do have a most significant, it's a work in process that takes constant nurturing. Some Micro-moves™ to consider are saying "I love you," leaving a sweet note, or saying "I'm sorry." You don't always need to be right, but you should always do your best to be a good listener.

🏃 TBE IN ACTION

Rob, Beth, and the Power of the Pink Book

Rob's most significant person is his wife, Beth, to whom he has been happily married for thirty-seven years. Both credit two Balance Equation™ practices with helping their relationship thrive. The first practice is writing in the pink book, a journal Rob writes in every morning and then shares with Beth. He explains, "This is a place where I share my feelings and emotions, what is going on with me, and gratitude for different things Beth helps me with. This practice was extremely helpful to both of us during my recent cancer diagnosis and the subsequent successful surgery.

Beth consistently reminded me even on my darkest days that 'We got this,' which was a tremendous help for me."

Beth comments, "The pink book is a private place where Rob shares his deepest self, gratitude for all that is good in our lives, and provides support for all our struggles. I always feel better after reading the daily entry and often write back a response, which reinforces that we are a team."

This practice is a Micro-move™ that takes Rob five to ten minutes to write and Beth no more than five minutes to read and respond.

Their second helpful Balance Equation™ practice is enjoying a weekly date night, something they've done every Wednesday night for the past thirty-seven years. Beth comments, "We both look forward to doing something together every Wednesday night. It breaks up the week and give us something to look forward to. It also reinforces the message that we are important enough to each other to shut out the rest of the world." Rob comments, "It was tougher to keep to the practice when our kids were growing, but we managed to do it with the help of family, friends, and great babysitters. Our weekly date night has allowed us to reconnect during the most challenging times."

This practice takes one to three hours each week, and Beth and Rob credit the Balance Equation™ for helping to reinforce that they are the most significant people in each other's lives.

It is important for all of us to consistently let the most significant people in our lives know this through Micro-moves™ like sending love you, thank you, and appreciate you texts and otherwise as mentioned above. Remember, you do not need to make a grand macro-move to let your most significant know that you appreciate them.

Family

Relationships = Most Significant + **Family** + Friends + Work + Inner Circle

The second category of relationships is family. In the traditional sense, family is a group of people related to you by blood or ancestry. This is the true meaning of family for some, but for others, family has nothing to do with genes and everything to do with unconditional love, compassion, and support.

Family relationships involve sharing goals, values, and long-term commitments. Much like friendships, family members give us the support we need to develop and reach our goals. Family members should make us feel heard and valued, which in turn helps us deal with stress or hardships, but family relationships develop and change over time, and it's completely normal to go through periods when we struggle or feel misunderstood by our family.

In many ways, our closest friends become our family throughout our lifetimes. Do you have people in your life you feel this intrinsic connection with? Practice life skills that deepen relationships such as listening, honesty, compassion, empathy, patience, and vulnerability and spend time with the people who make you happy. Learn more about who they are and allow them to learn about you. When you invest in healthy relationships with the people in your life, you are likely to build bonds as strong as traditional familial bonds can be. Also, remember that pets can be, and often are, family.

Who do you consider family? Do you feel good about the time you allocate to your family? It's not all or nothing. Micro-moves™ can be very impactful, such as calling or texting just to say hi. No matter how you do it, staying connected is good for you and your family members, and strengthening your family bond doesn't have to be difficult. Many different enjoyable activities can create happy memories, help you get to know each other better, and let you experience the world in new ways. For example, consider making a family-nurturing Micro-move™ from the list below.

FAMILY MICRO-MOVES™

- Get a board game out of the closet or purchase one for an evening of fun.
- Grab some food and have a picnic at the nearest park.
- Plan a movie night at home with popcorn and healthy snacks.
- Get in the car and drive together with no destination in mind.
- Spend an hour gazing at old family photographs.

Memories play a big role in strengthening family relationships, so keep adding them. In fact, research shows that after engaging in nostalgic reflection, people feel more socially valued, loved, confident, and optimistic.

Friends

Relationships **=** Most Significant + Family + **Friends** + Work + Inner Circle

Friends, the third category of relationships, are essential for a variety of reasons. For one thing, friends help us learn. Without childhood friendships to instigate the learning process and adult friends to maintain lifelong learning, it's hard to practice social skills such as forgiveness, empathy, laughter, kindness, and curiosity. These life skills are essential to self-development and are greatly improved by maintaining friendships.

Today Show anchor Hoda Kotb even believes, "You're the sum total of the five people you spend the most time with. Choose your friends wisely."

Most importantly, without friends, our support system can be minimal. You might feel unheard and undervalued, which in turn might make it harder to deal with stress or hardships. A support system is integral to survival. Without friends, you might have a harder time reaching your goals because of a lack of encouragement or people to hold you accountable. Research from Mayo Clinic highlights the fact that friendships support our total health.

 TBE EXERCISE

Assess Your Relationships

Take the assessment below. For the moment, ignore the QR code. Ponder the smiley faces and circle how you feel as you answer the following question: how do you feel about the time you put into your friendships?

Now list five friends below and the most recent date you had contact with them

Name   **Date**

1. _____   _____

2. _____   _____

3. _____   _____

4. _____   _____

5. _____   _____

If making this list was more difficult than you expected it to be, you aren't alone. Many of us get caught up in our day-to-day affairs and forget to nurture our friendships. A few Micro-moves™ will go a long way towards building and maintaining your friendships. Here are a few to consider:

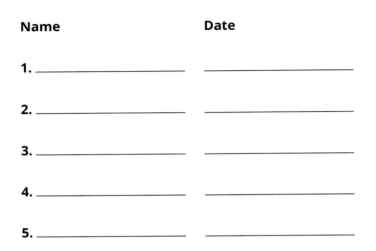

FRIENDSHIP MICRO-MOVES™

- Make a call.
- Send a text or picture.
- Set a time to get together.

The most long-lasting relationships are made with people you have common interests with. Joining a club, taking a class, or volunteering are good ways to meet new friends. This is why many of us become part of online communities to share our common interests. As discussed in chapter one, we created the Balance Equation™ Community for members to share experiences including Micro-moves™ and best practices. Finding people who enjoy the same activities as you is key because relationships are strengthened and maintained by experiencing things together. In other words, a friendship is more likely to last if you enjoy the same activities or have similar lifestyles.

If you are a current community member, log in. If you're not, use the QR code below to join now.

 Open up the camera on your phone and scan the QR code, which will bring you to a menu. Click on "Get Your Balance Number Now!" to take the assessment.

Good friendships require the investment of quality time. Our friends need to know that they are a priority to us and vice versa. When friends invest time, relationships deepen and grow.

Work

Relationships = Most Significant + Family + Friends + **Work** + Inner Circle

Most of us spend a significant portion of our lives working, typically forty percent of our waking hours, so work is also an important component of relationships. Whether you have a 9:00–5:00 office job or are a work-from-home mom or dad, work relationships take conscious effort and a time commitment. Whether you work in a physical office or virtually, it's important to connect with coworkers.

Our work relationships ebb and flow depending on a variety of factors, but these relationships are crucial to creating and maintaining a success-ful work environment. You don't have to be friends with everyone you work with—you don't even have to like everyone you work with—but you do have to be able to get along and get things done, despite personal or occupational differences. Being uncomfortable with the people you work with can lead to an unpleasant work environment, which can significantly impact your mood and mental health.

Don't Overstay Your Welcome

Working with someone you're incompatible with can be challenging, but it's definitely not impossible. Work relationships are built on mutual respect. Open communication is a crucial life skill that will not only help you develop respect for your work partner but will also help you compromise with someone who works differently than you. Make every effort to make your partnerships work, but if you've exhausted all possibilities, know when to cut the cord. Identify your needs by asking yourself the following questions:

- What are essential elements for you to be able to get this work or project done?
- Do you need to meet regularly with your work partner?
- Do you need to work alongside your work partner?

Learning about the coworker you struggle with can be an effective way to understand this person more deeply. If they've been negative or snappy, it's possible that something in their personal life is causing them to behave this way. This detail doesn't excuse rude behavior, but it can help you understand where they're coming from, which can make it easier to understand their needs and get work done with them.

Because good work relationships positively impact other areas of our lives, try incorporating a few of the following work-related Micro-moves™ into your day.

☝ WORK MICRO-MOVES™

- Say "Good morning" and "Goodbye" to your coworkers.
- Congratulate one of your coworkers on an accomplishment.
- Check in and ask how they are doing if you know they are struggling with a challenge in their lives.

Inner Circle

Relationships = Most Significant + Family + Friends + Work + **Inner Circle**

The final relationship category is composed of your inner circle. Your inner circle is made up of your go-to peeps, the people you consider your trusted advisors, those with whom you feel safe sharing sensitive information because you won't be judged. These individuals are your personal advisory group, a sounding board that might include family, friends, clergy, professors, mentors, coaches, doctors, lawyers, financial advisors, a current or former boss, or others you trust. Your inner circle might include your best friend's Uncle Vinny if he's an attorney or financial advisor you consult before buying a house.

The point is, these individuals give you an independent viewpoint and have your best interests in mind. The relationship is usually mutual; they feel comfortable coming to you too. While they often cross all passages in your life from childhood to adulthood, members of your inner circle may change over time as your life and needs change. This is why acquaintances, colleagues, and advisors sometimes evolve into members of your inner circle.

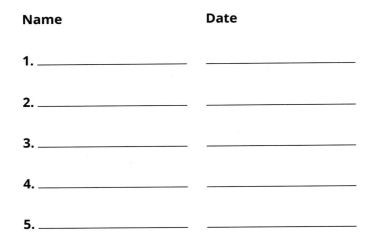 TBE EXERCISE

Assess Your Inner Circle

Who's in your inner circle? Are you investing time in these important relationships? List five people in your inner circle and the last time you communicated with them.

Name   **Date**

1. _____   _____

2. _____   _____

3. _____   _____

4. _____   _____

5. _____   _____

Now that you've listed these individuals, it's important to realize that you'll likely go to different members of your inner circle based on the specific life issue you're dealing with. You might be more comfortable discussing health matters with one individual, another for relationship issues, another with money concerns, and so on. It's useful for all of us to think about who we will go to if certain issues arise in our lives.

Micro-moves™ can let the members of our inner circle know we value them. Try one of the following or add your own.

☝ INNER CIRCLE MICRO-MOVES™

- Text, call, or email to check in.
- Let the people in your inner circle know they're in this circle.
- Respond promptly to your inner circle's texts, emails, and check-ins.

Other Inner Circles

Other inner circles might include a religious or cultural group, a club, a volunteer group, and so on. If you're an avid reader, a book club could be an example of an inner circle for you. It's important to have at least one inner circle no matter your age because it helps to reinforce your identity.

Many of the relationships we develop in our lifetimes (friends, family, significant other, work relationships) are innately reciprocal. That's not to say your inner circle relationships aren't. However, the point of having an inner circle is to help reinforce your identity.

Advisory Groups

Advisory groups are a good example of a group of people who reinforce the identity of others. A few of the better known business advisory boards are Young Entrepreneurs Organization (YEO), Young Presidents Organization (YPO), and Vistage. Rob was a member of Young Presidents Organization (YPO), a global leadership community of chief executives driven by the belief that the world needs better leaders. Through YPO, people come together to be inspired and supported to make a difference in businesses and lives throughout the world.

Rob's current advisory group, the Sockem Dogs (named after a spectacular whitewater rapid), is a group of twelve men and women who are no longer part of YPO but have continued to meet for more than thirty years. Members of YPO are exceptional leaders who have achieved significant leadership success at a young age and are at the top of their field, business, or organization. Each brings a diverse background of expertise, culture, and ideas and a thirst for knowledge and learning through programs and shared experiences. The result is an extraordinary inner circle whose members offer one another a safe harbor sounding board of trust and confidentiality that encompasses both business and personal issues. To Rob, these relationships are priceless.

If you have an inner circle relationship that needs to be worked on, make a Micro-move™ to improve it. Continue to think about what you can do to make that change. See if you can pick out or nurture some key activities or characteristics that are important to your sense of being. Remind yourself of what connects you on a deeper level to all your relationships.

 **TBE EXERCISE**

Assess Your Relationships

Now that you've learned about relationships and the five sub-categories (significant others, family, friends, work, and inner circle), think about how you feel about these relationships in your life. Ponder the smiley faces below and assess you how feel in the various subcategories of relationships.

| | 1 | 2 | 3 | 4 | 5 |

Relationships

Most significant	1	2	3	4	5
Family	1	2	3	4	5
Friends	1	2	3	4	5
Work	1	2	3	4	5
Inner circle	1	2	3	4	5

Add your number from each subcategory and record it below.

Total for Relationships: _____

This total number is how you currently feel about your relationship category.

Choose your lowest number from the subcategories above, then circle and begin one Micro-move™ from the list below. As always, feel free to add your own Micro-moves™ if you are so inclined.

☝ ADDITIONAL RELATIONSHIP MICRO-MOVES™

Significant Other
- Plan a date night with your most significant other or spouse.
- Text "I love you" to your spouse or significant other.
- Take the initiative to do a chore like washing the dishes or taking out the trash without being asked.

Family
- Go on an unplanned family picnic with whatever's in your fridge.
- Call/text a family member for no reason.
- Acknowledge birthdays and other important events.

Friends
- Call or text a friend to meet for coffee.
- Ask a friend to go to the gym or take a class.
- Tell a friend you appreciate them.

Work
- Check in with a coworker for no reason.
- Connect with a coworker by asking a question such as what their favorite food is.
- Recognize a coworker's contribution to a project or meeting.

Inner Circle

- Make a list of at least three people who are in your inner circle.
- Call/text a member of your inner circle to show your appreciation.
- Introduce a member of your inner circle to someone new.

RECAP

Relationships = Most Significant + Family + Friends + Work + Inner Circle

If you don't feel good about your relationships, then all the other major categories (self, health, and money) are affected. When you want to make a change in your life, once you truly know what's important for you, make a Micro-move™ to begin that change. How do you feel about your relationships? Eliminate autopilot by staying conscious about how you feel. How you spend your time should reflect your priorities. Remember:

- Healthy relationships share key characteristics such as trust, respect, affection, and openness.
- Relationships are enormously important for health, and many studies highlight the biological processes that account for the link between relationships and health.
- Healthy relationships take constant nurturing that can be achieved with small gestures.
- Many of us talk ourselves into perfection, which often leads to procrastination that results in a missed opportunity to express our true thoughts and feelings towards others.

- Create time for the most significant people in your life. Schedule this time. Block it on your calendar.
- The most significant person in your life is exactly that: the person you consider to be your highest priority no matter what.
- Many different family activities create happy memories.
- Research highlights the fact that good friendships support our emotional health.
- Our work relationships ebb and flow depending on our work environments and projects.
- Your inner circle consists of your go-to peeps, the people you consider your trusted advisors.

Now that you have a deeper understanding of relationships, one of the four major categories of the Balance Equation™, let's move on to the next chapter and explore money.

A Deep Dive into Money

The Balance Equation™ = Self + Health + Relationships + **Money**

Remember, time is money.

—Benjamin Franklin

Money is one of the four main categories of the Balance Equation™. If you don't feel good about money, then all the other categories (self, health, and relationships) are affected.

Money = Basic Expenses + Savings + Debt + Retirement + Charity

The subject of money tends to bring up many emotions and feelings. Indeed, "Ninety percent of Americans say money impacts their stress level," says consumer finance and money reporter Alexandria White of CNBC. While many people chase the almighty dollar, others are content with having enough to pay the bills. There is no right or wrong; the importance we place on money is a personal choice. We have seen many unhappy people who are wealthy and many happy people who have extremely modest resources. Most of us fall somewhere in between.

Research shows no direct correlation between income and happiness after achieving a certain level of income that allows us to meet basic needs. More specifically, once an income of $50,000 to $75,000 is achieved, wealth makes hardly any difference to overall well-being and happiness. If anything, it only harms well-being as evidenced by the fact that extremely affluent people suffer from higher rates of depression.

Most of us understand the money we have coming in but do not fully understand where it goes. The main reason is that few of us learn how to manage our finances. If you're lucky, you've received direction from a parent, a mentor, or have taken a course in personal finance, but according to financial services company Charles Schwab, seventy-two percent of U.S. households do not have a written plan to help them navigate their finances. This means most of us fly by the seat of our pants when it comes to money. Naturally, emotions flare due to this lack of knowledge and understanding.

How do you feel about money? Do you have enough to pay your bills? Are you always worried about money? Do you squabble with your significant other over money? Are you uncomfortable talking about money?

Take a look at the chart below and assess how you feel about money right now, in this snapshot of time.

No matter your number, take heart: you *can* get on top of your finances. It takes time, effort, discipline, and consistency, but it's worth it to avoid the ongoing stress caused by financial problems. The best move you can make if your number is lower than a 4 or 5 is to gain clarity on your current financial position. In the era of credit and debit cards, many of us are used to spending without tracking, so how do we gain clarity?

While there are all kinds of apps that track spending, sometimes a simple spending log on a sheet of paper is all you need. Of course, if you like, you can also use a spreadsheet. The same approach applies to all five subcategories: basic expenses, savings, debt, retirement, and charity. It's important to gain clarity on what you earn, spend, save, owe, and give of your time and money, and it all begins with taking care of the basics, so let's delve into the subcategories, starting with basic expenses.

Basic Expenses

Money = **Basic Expenses** + Savings + Debt + Retirement + Charity

Everyone has basic expenses, what some call their monthly nut, necessities, or must-haves to keep living. Housing (rent or mortgage), food, medical care, transportation, or utilities are examples of what most people consider basic expenses. For some of us, our meditation app, Peloton membership, Amazon Prime, Netflix, daily coffee, gym membership, club memberships, trips to the beauty parlor, manicures/pedicures, lessons, training, or massages are basic expenses. How much time do you spend thinking about where your money goes?

Research highlights that most people spend very little if any time tracking their finances.

In fact, only three percent of Americans spend time on household financial management on an average day, and on average, Americans spend fewer than two minutes a day managing their household finances.

Understanding your basic expenses is imperative if you wish to reduce your financial stress. Keeping a budget worksheet like the one on the next page can offer clarity. Without clarity, you may tell yourself tales based upon your feelings, and feelings can be deceptive. You might tell yourself, "I can afford this," "I deserve this," "I'll be able to pay for this later," or "I have a bonus or refund check coming." You might be right, but you might very well be wrong.

As a general rule, you should not spend money in advance of having the money. And while this may sound basic, living within your means allows you to know that your basic expenses will be covered every month.

Ultimately, it's vital to know your basic expenses so that you can make Micro-moves™ that accelerate your progress with money. Some actions that will help you keep track of your basic expenses are as follows:

BUDGET WORKSHEET

	BUDGET	
	PAYCHECK	+$
	RENT	−$
	UTILITIES	−$
	CELL PHONE	−$
	FOOD	−$
	TRANSPORTATION	−$
	MEDICAL	−$
	ENTERTAINMENT	−$
	CLOTHES	−$
	CREDIT CARDS	−$
	SURPLUS/ DEFICIT	± $

☝ BASIC EXPENSES MICRO-MOVES™

- Buy a small notepad to track your daily expenses.
- Always get a receipt and add your expenses into whatever tracking log you use.
- Review your expenses weekly to be conscious of where you stand.

 TBE EXERCISE

Gain Clarity on Your Basic Expenses
Mark your basic expenses from the following list with a "B." The remainder of the list should be discretionary expenses, or those expenses that are over and above what you consider to be necessities:

- Housing or rent
- Utility bills
- Cell phone
- Transportation and car insurance
- Food and groceries
- Childcare
- School costs
- Clothing and personal upkeep
- Pet food and care
- Health, life, and homeowners insurance
- Memberships and subscriptions

- Entertainment
- Credit card debt
- Loans
- Travel
- Retirement
- Emergency fund
- Large purchases
- Taxes

Many of us spend unnecessary time being anxious, even unable to sleep, because we are worried about meeting our financial obligations. However, the truth is often very different from the story we tell ourselves. With increased clarity and a more structured budget, over time, you can find yourself in better financial shape than you might have expected. When you feel confident about managing your basic expenses, you will likely experience tremendous benefits.

Don't Be Overwhelmed by the "B" Word

"B," in this case, stands for "budget." The mere sound of this word is enough to make most people anxious. However, a budget is nothing more than a personal spending plan. Once you have clarity over your earnings minus your basic expenses, the remainder of your money is discretionary. This can be a fun game to play. The coffee-a-day expense as shown in the graphic on the next page adds up very quickly. If you purchase a $5.00 cup of coffee every day for 365 days, you will spend $1,825.00. If you make your own coffee at home, you will spend about $182.50. You then end up with $1,624.50 of additional discretionary money to spend.

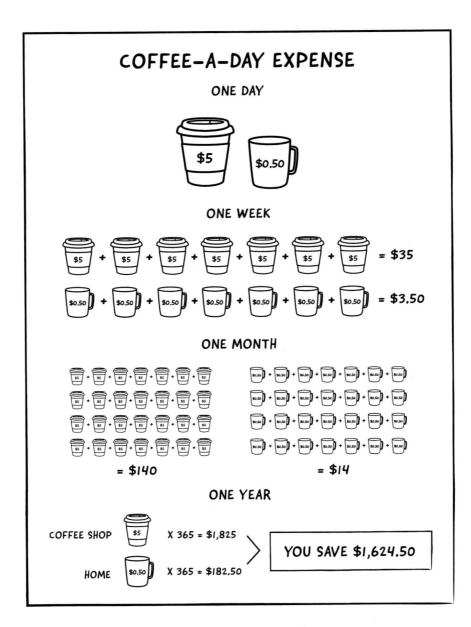

That said, balancing your basic expenses can be incredibly challenging if you spend money in an unstructured manner or do not have a regular income. The first step to creating a budget is knowing exactly how much money you make and spend each month. This process can be challenging, but keep in mind that you can and should amend your budget based on your current financial situation. After all, most people's budgets change and develop over time just like the economy changes and develops over time. Money isn't static, so learning how to balance changes helps us be more financially secure regardless of what happens.

Debt

Money = Basic Expenses + **Debt** + Savings + Charity + Retirement

While we all have basic expenses, most people also have debt to consider. Typically, the most significant debts are long-term obligations such as mortgages but long-term leases on an apartment or home are also debt, since your personal guarantee and/or a security deposit is usually required. Other long-term obligations include car payments, business loans, student loans, IRS payment plans, and other payment plans. Since it's always comforting to know we aren't alone on our money journey, consider this fact: as of the third quarter of 2021, the total debt of U.S. households was $15.2 trillion. Mortgage debt was $10.4 trillion, representing the largest component of long-term debt, and next came student loans at $1.6 trillion. All of these numbers continue to increase annually and are vitally important. Remember the quote from Peter Drucker in chapter one? "What gets measured gets managed." With that said, let's take a look at how to manage your debt.

Managing Debt

The first step to managing debt is to know how much you owe and to whom. Make a list of your debts, including the creditor, total amount of debt, minimum monthly payment, and due date. Writing things down helps you see your situation more clearly and allows you to be more organized when managing your finances.

Do you know how much debt you have? Here's a little secret: most of us don't know and some of us don't want to know. Debt is frightening, and we'd rather keep our heads in the sand. The truth is, clarity on our debts as well as our basic expenses is liberating, even if writing down our debts isn't that fun. Fun or not, use the following debt worksheet, put the figures in a spreadsheet, purchase an app, or write them down on a piece of paper. However, you do it, just do it.

While this exercise might seem more painful than it's worth, many people are late on their payments because they aren't clear on the due dates or simply forget them altogether. Clarity and organization allow us to make our payments on time and avoid late fees. That's important in a society that's heavily reliant on debt. Those who don't manage their debt properly often find their financial burdens morphing into a deeply emotional experience that negatively impacts all the other Balance Equation™ categories (self, relationships, and health). Debt that is out of control can create a downward spiral that continues to worsen unless and until you gain clarity and create a plan to dig out. With clarity on what we owe, when it is due, and how we will repay it, we get closer to rebalancing. And even if we can't repay debt now, we can create a plan to do so and begin chipping away at it.

DEBT WORKSHEET

TYPE OF DEBT	CREDITOR	BALANCE	MONTHLY PAYMENT AMOUNT	MATURITY DATE
MORTAGE/LEASE				
HOME EQUITY LOAN				
STUDENT LOANS				
AUTO				
CREDIT CARD				
PERSONAL LOANS				
OTHER:				
OTHER:				
OTHER:				
TOTAL		$ _____	$ _____	

Unfortunately, debt can strain relationships, not only among couples but also with others if we ask friends, family members, or those in our inner circle for loans. Without question, it can be incredibly challenging to navigate relationships when finances are involved. Having little to no debt or having a satisfactory payment plan gives us the structure we need to feel secure, freeing us up to live more balanced lives.

If you're in debt, try these debt Micro-moves™:

☞ DEBT MICRO-MOVES™

- Set up calendar reminders to pay your bills on time.
- Set-up auto payments for recurring payments.
- Pay more than the minimum payment whenever possible, even if it's just an extra $5.00 per month.
- Consolidate higher interest payments by transferring balances when possible.
- Eliminate credit cards that have annual fees.

Savings

Money = Basic Expenses + Debt + **Savings** + Retirement + Charity

Many of us are so concerned with our basic expenses and debt that we don't make time to think about savings. While saving may seem elementary, most people know they need a savings plan but do not have one.

According to GOBankingRates' 2019 survey, almost seventy percent of Americans have less than $1,000 in savings, and *forty-five percent of Americans have no savings at all.*

As mentioned earlier, our stress levels increase when we have no funds to cover unplanned expenses such as medical bills, car repairs, home repairs, or the loss of a job. Having the funds available to cover these types of expenses provides peace of mind.

Do You Have an Emergency Fund?

If your answer is yes, bravo. If your answer is no, you can start your emergency fund with as little as $10 per week (the equivalent of two cups of store-bought coffee), which will add up to more than $500 by the end of one year. The dollar amount of your emergency fund is a personal choice and does not need to be accumulated all at once. The key is to start small so there's no major impact on the quality of your life. This fund should not be used for anything other than unforeseen expenses.

Start small and pay yourself first. This can be accomplished with a variety of Micro-moves™ such as those listed below.

☝ EMERGENCY FUND MICRO-MOVES™

- Set a payroll deduction to put away a set dollar amount per paycheck. You will be amazed at how quickly this adds up.
- Any time money shows up, throw it into a jar, box, or envelope.
- Set up a separate emergency account that you do not touch for any other purpose.

Do you have any savings? Do you feel you are saving enough? Consistently saving money can be challenging, particularly if you're a spender, but it's a key component to financial balance. It gives you peace of mind and allows you to worry about one less thing, which can help improve your mental and emotional health. Having money isn't imperative for a fulfilling life, but understanding money is crucial for balance, and saving is one of the most basic skills that can give you the security, eventually, to do more.

THE MAGICAL PENNY

$2000 Cash or a Penny? What if the penny wasn't ordinary, but was magical?

The magical penny will DOUBLE IN VALUE every day for 31 days straight. Now which one would you choose?

Follow the path of the penny bellow to see if you made the right choice.

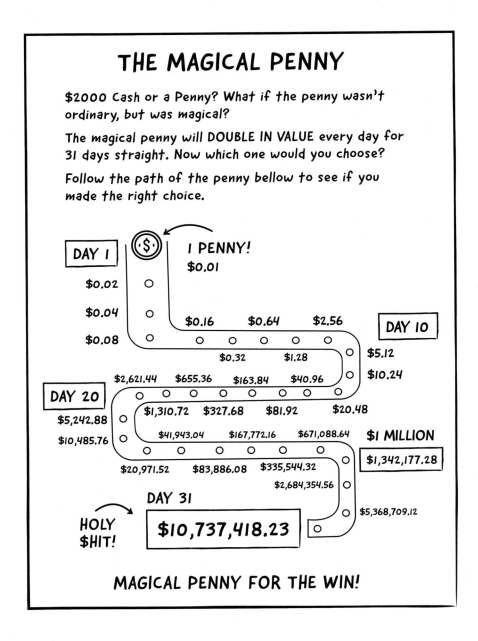

MAGICAL PENNY FOR THE WIN!

Depending on how you feel about money and the personal circumstances you find yourself in, it might be important to reframe your mindset about saving. Instead of simply spending less, which can feel vague and misguided, it might be motivating to find something to save for. Whether it's your education, a car, retirement, or something else, giving yourself something to work towards is a helpful psychological tool. However, remember to think big but start small. Saving is a cumulative process, and growing your savings happens over time.

A great example of the power of saving is shown in the concept of the Magical Penny, which was illustrated in an article from *Forbes* magazine in 2019. The Magical Penny, shown on the previous page, is an example of how engaging in Micro-moves™ consistently over time can create extraordinary results.

Now that you've started saving, let's dive into saving for when you stop working, otherwise known as retirement.

Retirement

Money = Basic Expenses + Debt + Savings + **Retirement** + Charity

How do you feel about your retirement? Do you have a retirement plan? Most people do not. Retirement can feel far off, especially if you're just starting out, but forty-one percent of Americans aren't addressing their retirement at all. Unfortunately, not planning for retirement can become a source of stress and financial burden for your family and friends, which can affect your relationships. One of the greatest gifts you can give your children is the freedom to not worry about how you'll support yourself in your old age.

Many people have a false sense of security regarding Social Security. Some even believe that Social Security alone will fund their retirement. According to usnews.com, as of January 2022, the average person's Social

THE POWER OF
COMPOUNDING INTEREST
AT 5% COMPOUNDING MONTHLY

START INVESTING... NOW VS. LATER

AGE	YEAR	BALANCE (rounded)	BALANCE (rounded)
20	1	$6,165	$0
25	6	$42,057	$0
30	11	$88,118	$0
35	16	$147,232	$0
40	21	$223,097	$0
45	26	$320,458	$55,693
50	31	$445,407	$139,763
55	36	$605,761	$247,656
60	41	$811,554	$386,121
65	46	$1,075,660	$563,821
70	51	$1,414,602 vs. $791,874	

TOTAL AMOUNT INVESTED: $312,000 vs. $384,000

Security check before income tax is $1,657 per month, or $19,884 per year. While this sum will cover some expenses, it isn't enough for most of us to live on. The amount that we receive depends on how much we have contributed to Social Security during our working years and the age at which we retire. For more information on Social Security, visit https://www.ssa.gov/.

Retirement plans may also include components such as an IRA, 401K, pension, annuities, insurance policies, and home equity. You may have already started one or more of these retirement savings vehicles. The key takeaway is that the sooner you start, the sooner you can take advantage of the power of compound interest, which works in everyone's favor no matter when you start. The chart on the previous page illustrates the power of compound interest and the advantage of starting early.

Regarding your eventual retirement, here are a few Micro-moves™ to consider:

☝ RETIREMENT MICRO-MOVES™

- Pay yourself first by setting a monthly contribution amount or percentage towards your retirement.
- Consult with a financial advisor or visit a retirement planning website.
- Be patient and consistent about saving.

⚡🏃 TBE IN ACTION

Meet Larry, Whose Retirement Planning Was Unparalleled

Stu's dad, Larry, was the quintessential example of thoughtful retirement planning. A humble man who took care of his family and a disciplined saver who took minimal risk, he lived within his means and didn't try to keep up with the Joneses. A trained mathematician, meteorologist, and systems engineer, he was all about programming for the best outcomes, so he knew that consistent accumulation and the magic of compounding worked. Employment with the same corporation (Litton Industries) for almost forty years allowed him to achieve balance and financial security. The company gave him the opportunity to buy savings bonds and shares of company stock from every paycheck. The $100 per paycheck he saved did not affect the family's lifestyle, and as time went on, he increased the amount but never took distributions before he retired. The magic of compounding meant these small (Micro-move™) amounts over almost forty years accumulated very substantially. This nest egg along with a company pension and social security allowed for a very nice and well-deserved retirement. Unfortunately, Larry died at age sixty-five, too early to fully enjoy the fruits of his labor, but Stu's mom, Sandra, reaped the benefits of the Magical Penny and is living a great life at the age of eighty-eight years young.

Stu wishes he'd followed his dad's great example when he first started working, but at the time he thought he had a better way. While he follows his dad's example today, he missed out on some of the benefits of compounding by not starting early.

Now that you've thought about how to balance your current spending with saving for your future, let's take a look at how you can help others.

Charity

Money = Basic Expenses + Debt + Savings + Retirement + **Charity**

Most people like to help others. This is a basic human need. However, it can be incredibly challenging to balance charity with the other money sub-categories. Charity isn't just about giving money; giving time is equally if not more valuable. If charity isn't a priority for you at this time in your life, it's okay to do nothing in this category and to feel good about it.

As mentioned earlier, if you're ready to incorporate charitable giving into your life, start small with Micro-moves™ that allow you to achieve your goals. Donate the amount that feels right to you. It's important to be mindful and not on autopilot when it comes to giving. Whether you give $5 or $5,000, there should be no judgment or expectation placed on financial donations. The purpose of charity is to help others but also to help yourself feel good about giving while not bringing on financial harm.

Giving our time can also feel good as long as it doesn't throw our other priorities out of balance. How much time do you want to allocate towards charity? While the answer is different for all of us, the answer might be "none" at this point in your life. It's important to think about this topic so that you are clear with yourself and alleviate any stress you might feel.

When you donate money, you are making the conscious decision to give your hard-earned pay to those who might need it more. This conscious decision, in many ways, is just as active and can be equally as helpful as donating time. The knowledge that you're helping others is hugely empowering and can make you feel happier and more fulfilled, which helps to improve the other categories within the Balance Equation™ such as self and health.

Why Giving Feels So Good

Can money buy happiness? It might, if you donate to a good cause. A great deal of scientific evidence shows that giving in practically any form has enormous benefits for the giver. This includes a happier mood, a greater sense of well-being, lower stress levels, lower blood pressure, and even better longevity.

More specifically, when you give money to a cause you believe in, your brain activity changes. According to a study published in the *Proceedings of the National Academy of Sciences*, there's a clear neurological basis for human altruism. Brain imaging studies show that giving generates increased activity in the brain's reward system. In other words, giving time or money enhances moods.

In fact, there are two areas of the brain that become more active when you give money to charity. The first is the mesolimbic pathway, the same area that distributes the feel-good dopamine chemicals associated with money and food. Giving is truly a natural high!

The second area activated by charitable giving is the subequal area of the brain, which plays a key role in formulating social attachment. In an age in which isolation and loneliness are all too common, giving to charity can serve as an important reminder that we're all interconnected and need to support each other.

In many ways, the rise of social media and the internet helps charitable donors develop even deeper feelings of connection. For example, donors no longer have to wait for the annual newsletter to arrive to find out how an organization used their funds. Instead, they can simply follow their favorite organizations on Facebook, Instagram, a website, and other places where nonprofits share information about what they're up to. The connection and resulting satisfaction are immediate and ongoing.

In addition to improving mental health, helping others can also have a positive impact on physical health. Participating in activities like volunteering and providing assistance to friends or family members can bring a wide range of benefits, everything from lower blood pressure to a lower mortality rate.

There are also many ways to help others that don't involve putting a drain on your finances, such as volunteering at food drives, animal shelters, passing out flyers, posting on social media, or emailing or calling local government officials about causes that are important to you. You can even choose to volunteer time or donate money by piggybacking on what other people or organizations are already doing. The important part of charity is that, in addition to supporting yourself, you make the conscious choice to support others in whatever way feels right.

This brings us back to the importance of assessing, evaluating, and prioritizing what is most important to you at this time in your life. How do you feel about charity? How does it fit into your life? Have self-compassion for whatever charitable donations you currently make, whether of money or time, and consider making some Micro-moves™, assuming these feel right to you and are financially responsible at this time in your life.

It's Okay Not to Give—Timing Is Important

You may feel that charity is important but do not have the time or money at this stage of your life. That's okay. Accordingly, give yourself a 4 or 5 in the charity subcategory of the TBE assessment. The important takeaway is that you feel good about not giving at this time.

☝ CHARITY MICRO-MOVES™

- Give one dollar each time you check out at your local market.
- Participate in an already established employer program (giving time or money).
- Mentor a student or someone else in need.

Because money can bring up both positive and negative feelings, it's important to be aware of our feelings towards money and to try to be objective in our decision making. Having a financial plan and budget that allows us to live within our means is an important first step. As mentioned earlier, being clear on both our inflows (money net income) and outflows (monthly and discretionary expenses) makes a difference. Living within our means is vitally important and reduces daily stress in our lives.

Now that you've learned about money and the five subcategories (basic expenses, debt, savings, retirement, and charity), try the exercise below.

● TBE EXERCISE

Assess Your Feelings about Money
Take the TBE assessment below. For the moment, ignore the QR code. Ponder the smiley faces and circle how you feel about money in each of the subcategories.

MONEY

Basic expenses	1	2	3	4	5
Debt	1	2	3	4	5
Savings	1	2	3	4	5
Charity	1	2	3	4	5
Retirement	1	2	3	4	5

Add your number from each subcategory and record it below.

Total for money: _____

This total money number is how you currently feel about money. Choose your lowest number from the subcategories above, then circle and begin one Micro-move™ from the list below. Don't forget to add additional Micro-moves™ if you are so inspired.

☞ ADDITIONAL MONEY MICRO-MOVES™

Basic Expenses
- Set calendar reminders so you pay your bills on time.
- Keep your bills in one spot.
- Routinely remove one or two items that you don't really need from your shopping cart.

Debt
- Make a list of credit card debt.
- Commit to paying one credit card off per month if possible.
- Use your debit card instead of a credit card.

Savings
- Set up an auto pay amount to save from each paycheck.
- Put your spare change in a jar (you might be surprised at how fast it adds up).
- Save more than $50 per week by making food, coffee, etc. yourself at home instead of purchasing it pre-made.

Charity
- Volunteer by giving your time to a local organization or charity.
- Choose one charity and make a donation you can afford.
- Donate some old clothes or other items that can help someone else.

Retirement

- List your retirement goals.
- Get clarity on how much money you will need to retire from an online retirement planning tool.
- Set up an autopay for a deduction every month for retirement.

RECAP

Money = Basic Expenses + Debt + Savings + Retirement + Charity

If you don't feel good about money, then all the other major categories (self, health, and relationships) are affected. When you want to make a change in your life, once you truly know what's important for you, make a Micro-move™ and begin that change. How do you feel about money? Eliminate autopilot by staying conscious about how you spend your money. How you do this should reflect your priorities. Remember:

- After a certain level of income, wealth makes hardly any difference to well-being and happiness.
- Knowing what you earn and spend relieves stress.
- It's liberating to have a spending/savings plan, so don't be overwhelmed by the "B" word.
- You always know your basic expenses are covered when you live within your means.
- Controlling your debt allows you more spending/savings options.
- An emergency fund provides a cushion for the unexpected as well as peace of mind.
- Saving, no matter how little, is a key component to financial balance.

- Starting small and paying yourself first is a good way to start a savings plan.
- Giving yourself an incentive to save for things like education, a trip, a special purchase, or special event is a great self-management motivational tool.
- Social Security is not enough to fund your retirement, and it may not be around in the future.
- The earlier you start saving for retirement, the more you benefit from the power of compounding.
- Giving your money or time, no matter how small, makes you feel better about yourself and life.

Now that you have a complete understanding of the four different categories of the Balance Equation™, let's move on to the next chapter and explore how you can shift your overall number and live your best life one Micro-move™ at a time.

Moving Your Overall Number with Micro-moves™

By working only when you are most effective, life is both more productive and more enjoyable. It's the perfect example of having your cake and eating it, too.

—Tim Ferriss

Now that you've worked through the four categories of the Balance Equation™, let's put it all together in the exercise below.

 **TBE EXERCISE**

Putting It All Together

Fill in your numbers from the online assessment and/or chapters three through six below.

Self + Health + Relationships + Money = Your Balance Equation™

_____ + _____ + _____ + _____ = _____

Congratulations! This Balance Equation™ number represents how you feel about all the major categories in your life. This number is unique to you. A snapshot of how you feel overall at this point in time, this number will change as you strive to align your priorities with how you spend your time. It will be useful to see how your number compares to others in the Balance Equation™ Community and comforting to understand you are not alone as you embark on this journey.

There is no perfect balance for anyone, but striving to continuously improve allows you to focus on what you feel is most important. How do you do this? Now that we've covered the four major categories of self, health, relationships, and money, let's put it all together. The Balance Equation™ process highlighted below allows you to continually improve in four easy steps.

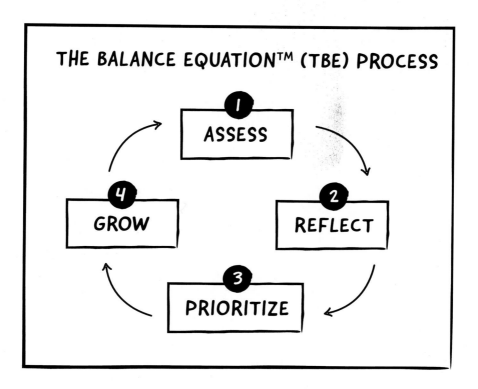

1. Assess your current state.
2. Reflect on where you are versus where you want to be.
3. Prioritize your Micro-moves™ based upon the areas you want to improve.
4. Grow by integrating your new Micro-moves™ into your routines.

This is an ongoing process that will continue to yield clarity and consciousness about how you feel. As Tony Robbins says, "Repetition is the mother of skill." The more you follow the TBE process, the more comfortable you will feel. Over time, hopefully, this process will become embedded in your routines, so let's revisit each of the four steps once again.

Congratulations—you've already assessed where you are. As mentioned in chapter two, most of us do not slow down enough to think about how we feel about the different categories in our lives. Continuously checking in and assessing our feelings allows us to be mindful and honest with ourselves. Be sure to practice self-compassion and acknowledge all feelings, both positive and negative, while you do this. We all have days that are good, bad, or in between. This is just part of the process.

Now that you know how you feel about where you currently are, make time to think about what is important to you and check in to see whether your vision aligns with your number. Most of us do not make the time to do this, but this life skill helps eliminate the conflict between how we want to live our lives and how we actually are living them.

Once you've reflected upon your current state, think about Micro-moves™ that can bring you into alignment with what is most important to you. This is where the TBE Prioritizer covered later in this chapter comes in. This tool highlights gaps between where you currently are and where you have opportunities for growth. Once you highlight the gaps, you can choose which Micro-moves™ to focus on now.

Once you choose a Micro-move™, add it to your routine and change will start to occur. Have self-compassion because change occurs over time, sometimes faster and sometimes slower than we like. Adding one Micro-move™ to your normal routine can bring immediate growth. Diedre Johnson's weight loss journey mentioned in chapter four started with the Micro-move™ of bringing home-prepped meals to work, which helped her lose more than 140 pounds and counting.

Continuous Improvement

Continuous improvement is, by definition, an ongoing process. There is no perfect balance for any of us, but following the TBE process allows us to move in the desired direction and continuously improve our lives and how we feel about them.

Let's look at an example. Ethan has just completed his assessment. Here are his numbers, with his lowest numbers highlighted in the TBE Prioritizer below

Ethan's TBE Prioritizer

SELF	18	HEALTH	15	RELATIONSHIPS	20	MONEY	21
Core values and beliefs	4	Physical	2	Most significant	4	Basic expenses	5
Personal time	3	Mental	4	Family	4	Debt	4
Development	4	Emotional	3	Friends	4	Savings	4
Work	4	Food	3	Work	4	Retirement	4
Spiritual	3	Sleep	3	Inner circle	4	Charity	4

Reflect: Ethan's lowest main category is health, which means there is opportunity for improvement. In general, Ethan doesn't feel particularly good about his health. When he dives deeper by looking at the five sub-categories of health, he sees that his lowest number is in the subcategory of "physical" with a 2.

Prioritize: Clearly, health is the area Ethan needs to focus on. Having made this decision, Ethan will choose a Micro-move™ from the list below to help him grow.

🤞 ETHAN'S HEALTH MICRO-MOVES™

- Schedule time to exercise today for five to ten minutes.
- Do strengthening exercises sometime during the day such as pushups or situps.
- Take a break from work and go for a walk.
- Use the stairs instead of the elevator.
- Always choose a parking space furthest from the entrance.

Grow: Ethan chooses a Micro-move™ from the health, physical, subcategory and begins to make physical movement part of his daily routine. How does he make it stick? Every morning when he wakes up, he stacks his habits by doing five pushups after he brushes his teeth. Habit stacking, according to James Clear in his book *Atomic Habits*, is the strategy of pairing a new habit with a current habit. In Ethan's case, brushing his teeth every morning is the existing habit he's been doing every morning for forty years. He stacks the pushups on top of the existing habit of brushing his teeth.

You can do what Ethan did. Take a few minutes to think about your current state, then do a new Balance Equation™ assessment or add in numbers based upon your assessments in the prior chapters. Fill in your lowest main category number and your lowest subcategory number. To make the process even more seamless, you can use the TBE Prioritizer below or download a printable version from the QR code that follows.

TBE Prioritizer

Circle your lowest main category.

SELF	HEALTH	RELATIONSHIPS	MONEY

Circle your lowest subcategory.

Core Values and Beliefs	Physical	Most Significant Other	Basic Expenses
Personal time	Mental	Family	Debt
Development	Emotional	Friends	Savings
Work	Food	Work	Retirement
Spiritual	Sleep	Inner circle	Charity

 Open up the camera on your phone and scan the QR code, which will bring you to a menu. Click on "Get Your Balance Number Now!" to take the assessment.

Then choose one or more Micro-moves™ from the list below (or create your own) and incorporate them into your life.

☝ ONE HUNDRED MICRO-MOVES™

Reduce social media time by five minutes a day.

Close your office door to reduce interruptions.

Reduce phone time by not picking up unknown numbers.

Write a sentence in a journal every day.

Make a list of the things you enjoy doing but don't have time for.

Eat lunch outdoors.

Remove the excess clutter from your desk.

Schedule time for self-care (a massage, manicure, pedicure, or facial).

Say good morning to everyone you come into contact with.

Learn something new every day.

Connect daily with friends and family.

Add time to your normal shower and enjoy!

SELF

Add a minute to breathe and focus on your breath.

Subtract a to-do-list item that is not urgent or important.

Read one page in a book or listen to a podcast for a few minutes.

Pick one skill you want to develop.

Join a new group like LinkedIn or your local chamber of commerce.

Learn a new computer skill.

Reach out to a colleague you don't know.

Take a walk during your break time.

List three things you are grateful for.

Spend time on prayer.

Reduce office interruptions.

Make your bed every morning.

Start a morning routine.

🤏 ONE HUNDRED MICRO-MOVES™

Reduce cardio time by five minutes to allow for strength or core training.

Do not hit the snooze button.

Engage in weekly meal preparation.

Meditate for one minute each day.

Do jumping jacks or pushups while your coffee brews in the morning.

Get up and do some stretching exercises.

Schedule exercise time.

Take a break and go for a walk.

Use the stairs instead of the elevator.

Schedule sleep time.

Listen to your favorite music.

Practice deep breathing for a minute when you get anxious or stressed.

Send a thank-you text to a coworker for a job well done.

Practice your listening skills during a Zoom meeting.

Tell a family member or friend that you love or appreciate them.

Drink a glass of water when you wake up.

Start your dinner thirty minutes earlier.

Keep a healthy snack like an apple or banana on hand at all times.

Turn off your devices before bed.

Drink a cup of chamomile tea before bed.

Reduce the room temperature by a few degrees.

Buy a jug to track your water consumption.

Carry healthy snacks.

Stop eating one hour earlier each night.

Make sure to laugh daily.

HEALTH

☝ ONE HUNDRED MICRO-MOVES™

RELATIONSHIPS

Subtract five minutes from your normal meeting times.

Reduce time spent with negative family members.

Subtract unproductive advisers from your inner circle.

Send a quick "thinking of you" text to a special someone or friend.

Go on an unplanned family picnic with whatever's in your fridge.

Call/text a family member for no reason.

Acknowledge birthdays and other important events.

Call or text a friend to meet for coffee.

Ask a friend to go to the gym or take a class.

Tell a friend you appreciate them.

Connect with a coworker by asking a friendly question such as their favorite food.

Recognize a coworker's contribution.

Make a list of at least three people who are in your inner circle.

Call/text a member of your inner circle to show your appreciation.

Introduce a member of your inner circle to someone new.

Send a thoughtful text to someone who needs encouragement.

Introduce one friend to another.

Invite a friend to a family event.

Do something special for someone just because.

Leave a thank you post-it note for someone.

Forward an article that relates to someone's particular interests.

Make donations in honor of someone.

Share an old picture of a memory.

Recommend something to connect.

☞ ONE HUNDRED MICRO-MOVES™

Subtract one Starbucks visit a week.

Subtract subscriptions for services you rarely use.

Eliminate your highest interest credit card.

Download an app that helps you track your spending.

Commit to paying down one credit card.

Make a list of your monthly expenses.

Review your expenses weekly.

Make a list of credit card debt.

Use your debit card instead of a credit card.

Set up an auto savings from each paycheck.

Make food, coffee, etc. at home.

Give your time to a local organization or charity.

Make an affordable donation.

Donate some old clothes or other items.

Give one dollar each time you check out at your local market.

Participate in an already established employer program (time or money).

Mentor a student or someone else in need.

List your retirement goals.

Choose one online tool to plan retirement.

Use discount coupons.

Join loyalty discount programs.

Research debt consolidation.

Shop at a discount store.

Review your credit card statements.

MONEY

Once you complete these four steps, congratulate yourself. You have completed the entire TBE process, perhaps for the first time. As you can see, it's simple and takes a minimal amount of time. You now have a framework to assess how you feel in all areas of your life. Continue the process of adding Micro-moves™ to the areas you want to improve and feel better about. Some Micro-moves™ will have an immediate impact while others will take longer to yield results. Be patient with yourself and have realistic expectations. Our more than thirty years of consistently applying this process and adding Micro-moves™ has improved our lives, not always in the time frame we expected, but with patience and perseverance, it has led us to happier lives. We are confident you will achieve similar results.

🏃 TBE IN ACTION

Alan Gets His Priorities Straight

Our friend Alan is a husband of forty-five years, a father of two, a grandfather of three, an early adopter of TBE, and a member of the Balance Equation™ Community. Once upon a time, while considering whether or not to take on a new job, he felt overwhelmed and out of balance. Consequently, he signed a contract without considering the consequences of the time commitment. In assessing the decision afterwards, he realized the new commitment would mean sacrificing core relationship time with his wife. Additionally, his physical and mental health were threatened by the added work stress. Thankfully, he paused, reflected, and decided to prioritize time with his wife. He then made a Micro-move™ to request fewer hours from his new employer and renegotiate his contract. With the Balance Equation™ to bolster him, he was prepared to lose the job, but his employer was willing to keep him on even though he would be working less.

Alan shared, "This was the outcome I'd hoped for, but far more importantly, I'd been paying attention and prioritized my current needs and values and consequently made a healthy decision. I definitely attribute this action to using the Balance Equation™."

RECAP

Self + Health + Relationships + Money = Your Balance Equation™

Keep these points in mind:

- There is no perfect balance for any of us.
- Continuously working the TBE process moves you towards living a life focused on what you feel is most important.
- As you incorporate Micro-moves™ into your life, your Balance Equation™ will change.
- Follow the Balance Equation™ process: assess, analyze, prioritize, grow.
- Prioritize your Micro-moves™ with the TBE Prioritizer.
- Realistic expectations and patience are the keys to growth and living your best life.

Now that you understand the TBE process and how to add Micro-moves™ to your life, let's move on to the next chapter and accelerate your growth.

Accelerating Your Growth and Getting to Flow

Your Balance Equation™ = Self + Health + Relationships + Money x Your Optimizers & Accelerators

Control of consciousness determines the quality of life.

—Mihaly Csikszentmihalyi, the Father of Flow

Chapters one through seven laid out the basic components of how to continuously improve and feel better about your life. This chapter delves into being fully conscious of your TBE numbers and what you want to change and shows you how to take your numbers to the next level with TBE optimizers and accelerators.

It's important to understand the difference between optimizers and accelerators. Optimizers are strategies that help you improve all your Balance Equation™ categories while accelerators are tools that help increase the speed of adoption in your life.

We are all looking to fast track or hack our way towards more immediate growth. TBE optimizers and accelerators allow us to compound our growth and do just that. Below, we explore specific optimizers that will maximize *your* results.

Optimizing Strategies

Optimizing strategies are all about your long-term success and making sure the Micro-moves™ you add stick. Our top five optimizing strategies follow below.

1. Embrace the TBE Mindset

A mindset is a fixed mental attitude or disposition that predetermines a person's responses to and interpretations of situations. It's important to have the right mindset for success in life. Victor Frankl wrote his landmark book *Man's Search for Meaning* after surviving the Holocaust in the notorious concentration camp Auschwitz in which he lost his wife, son, and many other family members. He had every reason to have a bad attitude. Instead, he chose to find the positive and good in the midst of extremely negative circumstances. He said, "Everything can be taken from a man but one thing, the last of human freedoms—to choose one's attitude in any given set of circumstances."

We all have a choice each day as to whether we will have compassion for ourselves and others and a positive attitude. Research from healthyplace.com highlights some of the following benefits of positivity:

1. Positive thoughts change the neural pathways in your brain.
2. Positivity makes you more receptive to learning.
3. Writing about positivity leads to better health.
4. Positivity helps you live longer.
5. Positivity leads to better cardiovascular health.
6. Positivity lowers your blood pressure.
7. Positive thinking boosts your immunity.
8. Positivity improves your social life because people gravitate towards other positive people.

Making the choice to be positive is up to each of us. We are all responsible for our own positivity or lack thereof. A simple Micro-move™ would be to adopt a positive attitude and mindset each morning. An affirmation such as "I am going to have a great day today and maintain a positive attitude" often helps anchor positive thoughts in our minds. So does the next optimizing strategy, practicing gratitude.

2. Practice Gratitude

Gratitude is an expression of appreciation for what we have. It helps people feel more positive emotions, relish good experiences, improve their health, deal with adversity, and build strong relationships.

Are you grateful for what you have? Oprah Winfrey says, "Be thankful for what you have; you will end up having more. If you concentrate on what you don't have, you will never ever have enough."

If practicing gratitude feels like a stretch, a gratitude journal can help. Writing down what we're thankful for raises our consciousness and creates positivity in our lives. Other simple ways to track gratitude include using a notes list on your phone or computer or thinking of all the things you are grateful for as you drift off to sleep each night.

Gratitude does not mean we disregard the bad things we experience, but focusing on the positives makes a difference. We all have challenges, but one person's struggles might be another person's opportunities, depending upon their mindset.

3. Be Mindful of the "F" Factor—Fun, Fear, Faith, and Focus

Fun

Regardless of your age, you should never stop having fun. Every action and activity can be fun if you have a positive attitude and the right mind-set. Achieving this desired state requires consciousness and making fun intentional.

Can you remember the last time you genuinely had fun? When was the last time you took a moment to put your responsibilities aside and do something fun? To live in the moment?

Don't hold back. Make time to have fun every day, if possible. This can include something as simple as enjoying a really good cup of coffee while sitting with your spouse, a family member, friend, your pet, or a colleague at work. It can be as simple as calling an old friend to catch up or watching your favorite television show. Block out thirty minutes every day to do something fun. Don't let anything hold you back.

Joy is closely related to fun. We can be more productive, creative, persistent, and even flexible when what we're doing brings us joy. Having fun can help us face our fears or problems, and this is something few people regret. Real fun makes you feel better inside and helps you realize if and when you need to make a change in your life.

If you have no idea what to do to have fun, sit down with a notebook and list the things you enjoy doing, anything from baking to watching funny movies to playing the harmonica, whatever makes you smile. While contemplating these small pleasures, trust the response you feel, such as your whole body relaxing. This is a powerful clue from your true self that you are awakening your sense of fun. Recognizing this physical change can point you to a more meaningful, joyful life.

Life should be fun, and it starts with ourselves. If fun is something you value, then you should try to bring fun to most things you do. Fun almost always starts with a positive attitude, as it's always more fun to be around those who are positive than negative. You might remember a sourpuss or two from your past who had a bad attitude, but most of us remember people who had positive attitudes. Be a self-styled fun ambassador and add joy and laughter to those around you. It will almost always be rewarded and appreciated.

 **TBE EXERCISE**

Lighten Up!

Think about the four categories of the Balance Equation™: self, health, relationships, and money. Grab a piece of paper or your phone and make a list of how you can add fun to each of these categories.

Take self. Do you listen to funny podcasts? Comedy Central? Read funny articles or books? If the answer is no, give any or all of these ideas a try.

Now look at health. Do you look forward to working out? Can you change up your fitness routine to make it more fun?

How might you do this? Let's assume you're already walking three days a week as part of your fitness routine. Why not change it up and make it more fun by adding music to your routine? Another fun option is to change up your walking location.

Now consider relationships. Do you make time to see family and friends? Are you thoughtful about checking in or congratulating those you care about when they experience disappointments or successes? Can you schedule a Zoom call or meet a friend at a new restaurant or show?

Finally, let's look at money. Do you make money a game? Try challenging yourself to see how much you can save today or this week. Consider joining an investment club such as CNBC Investing Club, Investment Clubs of America, or Value Investors Club. Keep coupons handy to use when shopping. Saving money is fun!

The real goal of having fun is to reap its benefits. Having fun isn't self-indulgent, nor should it be looked at as trivial, because it's actually one of the bravest things you'll ever do. After all, we tend to take unexpected, unique, and interesting turns when we do what thrills us the most. Along the way, we'll be challenged, questioned, and stretched to our limits but also gratified beyond belief.

"You never know unless you try" is a true statement of bravery as you break down your fears, so let's take a closer look at fear as well as the other two "F" factors.

Fear

A lot of us hold back from trying something new, such as a new relationship or job, because of fear. Your consistent use of the Balance Equation™

will help you make changes through Micro-moves™ that lessen your fear of trying something new. While fear is real, it's usually unfounded. As Napoleon Hill, author of the famous book *Think and Grow Rich*, said, "Fears are nothing more than a state of mind."

Some people fear success as much as they do failure. They often think success will leave them swamped or overwhelmed by too much work. Other common fears include the following:

1. Fear of public speaking
2. Fear of changing jobs
3. Fear of entering or leaving relationships
4. Fear of going to new places
5. Fear of trying new things
6. Fear of others' opinions
7. Fear of injury
8. Fear of bad news
9. Fear of opening and paying bills

But here's the good news: the fear of perceived negative outcomes is often much worse than the reality. We fear the unknown and make up stories in our heads based on information we don't have clarity on. That's why it's so vital to be conscious of what is real. You can conquer fear with the faith that there is always a solution.

Faith

Hope is a healer that shows us how to act, have belief in ourselves, and enjoy inner peace. British historian Thomas Carlyle once said, "He who has health, has hope, and he who has hope has everything."

Living your life with faith and working to see the glass half full helps us have a positive attitude. We all believe in different things, but if we have faith in ourselves, we can conquer anything. Faith in the universe and in our family and friends is vital, but the most important faith is the faith in ourselves, and this is where affirmations come into play. Here are some examples of affirmations:

- I'm ready to face the challenges of today.
- I am grateful for my life.
- Today is filled with opportunity.
- I am great.
- I am strong and healthy.
- I trust my inner wisdom.
- I begin the day with peace and gratitude.
- This day is filled with possibilities and potential.

You are more likely to have a great day if you tell yourself you are going to have a great day. Telling yourself, "I will meet my goals" can help you do just that. Using affirmations is a Micro-move™ that can help you accomplish more than you realize because affirmations set the tone for your day and your life. Napoleon Hill, again in *Think and Grow Rich*, talks about the power of auto suggestion, which is a way to remind ourselves that we can accomplish anything. The more we affirm what we can do, the greater chance we will keep it top of mind and work to accomplish it. This is a positive loop for success.

Focus

In an article titled "Why Multitasking Is a Myth, Backed by Science," Barbara Oakley, professor of engineering at Oakland University in Michigan, says, "Multitasking is like constantly pulling up a plant. This kind of constant shifting of your attention means that new ideas and concepts have no chance to take root and flourish."

We all have times in the day when we're most productive. These time slots are different for all of us. You may be more of a morning person, afternoon person, or evening person. The key is to understand when you're at your most productive. Naturally, people are more productive when they do their most important work during their most productive times each day, so it's important to block these productive time slots and work on your highest priorities.

To get into deep focus, we must eliminate all distractions. In addition, we do our best work when we focus on one thing at a time. Gary Keller in his book *The One Thing* highlights that we should always do our most important things first. When are your most productive times of the day? Do you know? Most of us don't stop to think about it, but it's very powerful to know when you are most productive so you can schedule your most important priorities, control your environment, and accomplish your "one thing." Determine your most productive time each day, find a quiet place, put away your phone, and focus deeply so that you can accomplish that most important "one thing."

In addition, try these quick pointers to achieve deep focus:

1. Schedule your "one thing."
2. Find a quiet environment, not a coffee shop filled with people and noise.
3. Eliminate distractions: turn off your phone and eliminate notifications on your computer.
4. Determine the amount of time to devote to achieving deep focus; a good starting point is twenty minutes.
5. Set a timer.

4. Subtract for a Net Positive

Many of us, when we want to improve our lives or health, initially try to add more to our days. While this might work to a certain extent, it can actually reduce our overall quality of life. In other words, sometimes we can improve our lives by subtracting what is not a current priority instead of adding more to our already full lives. The concept of subtracting can be applied to every area in the Balance Equation™ through Micro-moves™.

MICRO-MOVES™ THAT SUBTRACT

SELF	HEALTH	RELATIONSHIPS	MONEY
Reduce social media time by ten minutes a day	Reduce cardio time by five minutes to allow for strength or core training	Subtract five minutes from your normal meeting times	Subtract one Starbucks visit a week
Reduce office interruptions	Reduce morning wakeup time by not hitting the snooze button	Reduce time spent with negative family members	Subtract subscriptions for services you rarely use
Reduce phone calls by not picking up unknown numbers	Reduce your consumption of unhealthy fast foods by prepping meals in advance	Subtract unproductive advisers from your inner circle	Eliminate your highest interest credit card

How do you subtract to have more fun, lose your fear, and increase your faith and focus?

- To improve your "self" category, eliminate unwanted responsibilities. For example, reduce the time you spend at work and in other obligations.

- To improve your health, change or stop unhealthy habits. For example, stop smoking and/or limit the amount of alcohol you drink.
- To address your relationship category, get out of a toxic relationship or make an effort to get along with a prickly coworker or neighbor.
- To improve your money category, sell unnecessary possessions or eliminate subscriptions you don't use.

The bottom line is, you can improve the quality of your life through subtracting, getting rid of useless activities, things, and even people who do not serve your highest good. Subtracting is about getting rid of everything that isn't important to you. In other words, less is more.

We all have twenty-four hours each day that can easily be wasted if we aren't careful. We have to decide and then focus on what is important to us. Sometimes, adding more things, people, or activities does not improve the quality of life. Simplicity can actually be more energizing and healing because we focus on our passions and the people and things we actually love.

Plan While You Subtract

According to Winston Churchill, "He who fails to plan is planning to fail." We who practice the Balance Equation™ are big believers in making time every day, week, and year to plan and schedule the important things in our lives, including when we're going to sleep, eat, work, and exercise. Having a plan allows us to make time for what is most important to us. Planning gives us control. When we create plans, we're able to make choices and decisions rather than leaving things up to chance, or, worse yet, letting others make decisions for us. A plan makes everything easier, but it's important to be flexible and to modify plans as needed.

In the book *Your 168: Finding Purpose and Satisfaction in a Values-Based Life,* author Harry Kraemer talks about being "planful." While many see planning as rigid, Kraemer says the opposite is true. Planning allows us to put our priorities first while allowing for spontaneity. Being planful combines planning with mindfulness. So how do you do this? Consider using an online calendar like Google Calendar or Microsoft Outlook that combines your personal and professional schedules in one place and includes reminders and notifications to maximize your efficiency. You can also accomplish the same goal with online or paper-based planning systems such as Franklin Covey or Day Timer.

5. Beware Procrastination

The word "procrastination" is derived from the Latin verb *procrastinare*, which means to put off until tomorrow. Sound familiar? A procrastination study by Darius Faroux of more than 2,200 working professionals found that 88 percent of the workforce and 76 percent of entrepreneurs procrastinate at least one hour per day. The cost per worker on average is at least $15,000 per year.

Perfectionists are often procrastinators who would rather avoid tasks they can't do perfectly than undertake them. Some procrastinate out of fear of making the wrong decision. Others procrastinate because they don't know which decision to make. Needless to say, putting off making decisions is a decision in and of itself, and this time waster negatively affects morale. Use Micro-moves™ to get around this fact of life and past procrastination.

PROCRASTINATION MICRO-MOVES™

- Schedule the "one thing" you need to finish each day first.
- Keep your workspace clear of distractions.
- Get up early.
- Go to bed early.

- Do your least pleasant tasks first.
- Do your most important tasks first.
- Keep a calendar or to-do list.
- Reward yourself when you finish an important task.
- Utilize an accountability partner or partners.
- Minimize distractors (turn off email and social media).
- Have compassion for yourself. We all procrastinate at times; the key is to minimize how often we do so.

According to the Life Hacks website, there are five types of procrastinators and five solutions. As you read the following section, assess yourself. Which type of procrastinator are you, and what are you willing to do about it?

Five Types of Procrastinators

Perfectionists are forever seeking the perfect time or approach. Action to consider: re-clarify your goals and what's truly important to you.

Ostriches are dreamers who prefer to stay in the dreaming stage. Action to consider: do difficult tasks first each day.

Self-saboteurs do nothing to avoid bad things happening. Action to consider: write out a daily to-do and not-to-do list each day.

Daredevils believe deadlines can push them to do better but that starting early will sacrifice their time for pleasure. Action to take: create a timeline with deadlines.

Chickens lack the ability to prioritize their work and like to fly by the seat of their pants. Action to take: break tasks into bite-sized pieces.

⫘ TBE IN ACTION

TBE Optimizers Helped Andrew Navigate Life-Changing Events

Stu's oldest son, Andrew, is thirty-two years old, has been married to his wife, Amy, for five years, is a father to a fifteen-month-old son, and has another son on the way. A corporate marketing executive with side gigs that support his multiple passions, he works and plays hard, engages in consistent daily workout routines, prepares healthy meals for the family, enjoys live music and new restaurants, and was an early adopter of TBE.

Four months ago, seeking a better, more balanced, life experience, Andrew moved his family across the country to Florida. He had everything all planned out and could taste it coming together. In fact, he and Amy had just told the family the good news that they were expecting their second son. But as mentioned earlier, despite our most careful planning, life is unpredictable. Four days after returning home from a family vacation, Amy was involved in a very bad car accident. Not only was there concern for Amy's life but also for the life of the unborn baby. An ambulance took her to the hospital while Andrew received the news via a call from a stranger. He made a choice early in the process to adopt a series of TBE optimizers that he says changed the game.

First, he deliberately embraced the TBE mindset. He committed to a positive mindset by following Victor Frankl's lead and choosing to find the positive and good in the midst of extremely negative circumstances.

Second, he practiced gratitude. He decided to focus on what he was grateful for such as Amy being alive and, later, that the unborn baby was okay. He had a lot of loving support from family and friends.

Third, he prioritized the F Factor—Fun, Fear, Faith, and Focus. Although he was afraid, he knew the only way to overcome this fear was with overall faith that everything was going to be okay. Focusing on Amy's well-being was the number one priority; everything else could be dealt with later. He also consciously embraced the Micro-move™ of doing something fun daily, such as playing with his son and the dog for five minutes.

Fourth, he subtracted. Knowing that he needed time to focus on his wife's health and family responsibilities, he subtracted work time by quickly taking a leave from his job.

Andrew shared, "The positive TBE mindset was the key to staying grounded during a very stressful time. When things didn't go as expected, such as when the doctors didn't communicate with each other and caused unnecessary delays, I wanted to scream out loud but kept my cool. This made everything better for Amy, our son Wes, our dog Theo, the rest of the family, and me."

Acceleration Strategies to Speed Your Progress

Accelerators allow you to speed up the progress you are making by using the Balance Equation™ process. We have utilized the following acceleration strategies in our practice, all of which advance results. Our favorite acceleration strategies include the following.

1. Using Micro-moves™

If you haven't already done so, add Micro-moves™ to your existing, already successful routines to strengthen areas where you're weak and want to improve. Consistency leads to confidence and results.

2. Bundling Micro-moves™

Bundling your Micro-moves™ changes up the concept of using individual Micro-moves™ by pairing two or more Micro-moves™ for compounded benefits. Experience shows this concept generates efficiencies. Here's an example: listen to a podcast that helps you develop in the self category while exercising to benefit your physical fitness in the health category.

3. Stacking Habits

Pairing a new Micro-move™ with an existing habit is what James Clear calls habit stacking. An example is drinking a glass of water before or after you make your bed. In other words, you add a health-related Micro-move™ to a habit you've already incorporated into your life. This technique will improve the "stickiness" of the new Micro-move™.

4. Saying No

It isn't reasonable to think we can do everything. Saying no is liberating. The fact is, we can't please everyone. Putting ourselves first allows us to be our best for others.

Building Momentum and Getting to Flow

The point of using optimizers and accelerators is to build momentum. This involves increasing the actions that move you forward and decreasing the ones that hold you back. In other words, building momentum requires taking action. According to businessman Conrad Hilton, founder of the Hilton Hotels chain, "Success seems to be connected with action. Successful people keep moving. They make mistakes, but they don't quit."

Like Micro-moves™ and Micro-move™ bundles, momentum is an accelerator that moves us toward living our best life. How do we build momentum?

We can take advantage of adding Micro-moves™ to one of our existing routines to create momentum. This acceleration occurs because we are building on our existing success. Many examples can be found across all categories of the Balance Equation™ (self, health, relationships, and money).

Success leads to a dopamine spike that feels good. Higher levels of dopamine can lead to feelings of euphoria, bliss, enhanced motivation, and concentration. Naturally, it's human nature to want to repeat these positive feelings.

We all know that feeling when we have momentum: the pieces come together and we click on all cylinders. Athletes describe this as being in the zone. Famed psychologist Mihaly Csikszentmihalyi called the experience flow. When we experience flow, he said in an interview with *Wired* magazine, "the ego falls away. Time flies. Every action, movement, and thought follows inevitably from the previous one, like playing jazz. Your whole being is involved, and you're using your skills to the utmost."

Flow occurs when we're completely engaged in a creative or playful activity. Research highlights that while we're in the state of flow, we experience an increase in brain activity that results from higher levels of dopamine.

Characteristics of Flow

According to Csikszentmihalyi, ten factors accompany the experience of flow, but it isn't necessary to experience all of them for flow to occur:

1. The activity is intrinsically rewarding.
2. There are clear goals that, while challenging, are still attainable.
3. There's a complete focus on the activity itself.
4. People experience feelings of personal control over the situation and the outcome.
5. People have feelings of serenity and a loss of self-consciousness.
6. There is immediate feedback.
7. The task is doable; there's a balance between skill level and the challenge presented.
8. People experience a lack of awareness of their physical needs.
9. There is strong concentration and focused attention.
10. People experience timelessness, or a distorted sense of time, that involves feeling so focused on the present that they lose track of the passing of time.

The Benefits of Flow

In addition to making activities more enjoyable, flow leads to a number of other advantages:

- **Better emotional regulation.** With increased flow, people also experience more growth emotionally. This can help them develop skills that allow them to regulate their emotions more effectively.
- **Greater enjoyment and fulfillment.** People in a flow state enjoy what they are doing more. Because the task becomes more enjoyable, it is usually rewarding and fulfilling.
- **Greater happiness.** Research also suggests that flow states may be linked to increased levels of happiness, satisfaction, and self-actualization, where personal potential is fully realized once basic bodily and ego needs have been fulfilled.

- **Greater intrinsic motivation.** Because flow is a positive mental state, it can help increase enjoyment and motivation. Intrinsic motivation involves doing things for internal rewards, not necessarily for external acknowledgement or rewards.
- **Increased engagement.** People in a flow state feel fully involved in the task at hand.
- **Improved performance.** Researchers have found that flow can enhance performance in a wide variety of areas, including teaching, learning, athletics, and artistic creativity.
- **Learning and skill development.** Because the act of achieving flow indicates a substantial mastery of a certain skill, people tend to continuously seek new challenges and information in order to maintain this state.
- **More creativity.** Flow states often take place during creative tasks, which can help inspire greater creative and artistic pursuits.

How Do We Achieve the State of Flow More Often in Our Lives?

Flow comes and goes for all of us. However, when we are conscious of why and how flow happens, we can focus on creating the conditions that allow us to reach this state more often. The entire Balance Equation™ process—access, reflect, prioritize, grow—is aligned with the characteristics of flow and is a tool to help us reach the ultimate state of flow more often.

RECAP

Your Balance Equation™ = Self + Health + Relationships + Money x Your Optimizers & Accelerators

Optimizers are strategies that help you improve all your Balance Equation™ categories while accelerators help increase the speed of adoption. Building momentum involves increasing the actions that move you forward and decreasing the ones that hold you back. Flow occurs when every action, movement, and thought follows inevitably from the previous one. The state of flow includes the feeling of complete engagement in a creative or playful activity and is often referred to as "being in the zone," "on fire," or "on a roll."

Now that you know the fundamentals of the Balance Equation™ and how to incorporate it into daily life, let's look at how to integrate Balance Equation™ routines into your daily practice.

TBE Routines

*You will never change your life until you change
something you do daily. The secret of your success
is found in your daily routine.*

—John C. Maxwell

A routine is the practice of regularly doing things in a fixed order, usually a series of things that you do at a particular time. Those of us who practice the Balance Equation™ believe in the power of routines. They allow us to accomplish our life priorities even when we don't feel like doing them. If you wake up late, for example, you are still likely to brush your teeth on your way out the door even if you are unlikely to complete a full morning routine. However, if you wake up on time or a few minutes earlier than usual, you are more likely to complete this full morning routine. Your actions define your life priorities, so if you feel resentful about not completing your priorities, then add them to your routine. They are more likely to be completed because routines add consistency. We do them even when we don't want to.

What do routines mean to you? What pops into your head when you think about routines? Do you have any routines? Are they healthy routines?

◗ TBE EXERCISE

Make It Routine
Grab a piece of paper or open a Word or Google document and list one routine you can't live without. It might be brushing your teeth, having a cup of coffee to start every day, or always making your bed as soon as you wake up.

A day in the life of Oprah Winfrey is filled with many routines, as she shared in the February 2018 issue of *Harper's Bazaar*. Some of these include brushing her teeth, enjoying nature, engaging in spiritual and physical exercises, eating dinner by 6:00 p.m., and taking a bath to end the day. Tony Robbins understands the importance of a morning routine. His includes a morning plunge into a fifty-seven-degree Fahrenheit pool for a "radical change in temperature." Author Tim Ferris shares the importance of morning rituals and routines in his book *The 4-hour Workweek*. This includes making his bed every morning, something he considers a personal achievement.

According to research from Tel Aviv University, predictable repetitive routines are calming and help reduce anxiety. They also help you take control of your day and subsequently your life. In addition, starting and ending your day with a routine:

- Puts you in control of your day
- Saves your brainpower for the most important decisions since the small decisions are part of your routines
- Helps you sleep better and wake up more refreshed
- Improves relationships by allowing you to enjoy quality time with the people you love, whether through regular shared meals, reading a story at bedtime, or something else
- Gives you more time for the activities you enjoy with scheduled self-time routines
- Enhances physical and mental health through exercise and meditation routines that can be included during your workday (for example, a morning break walk, a walk after lunch, or meditation resets your mind for the rest of the day)

In developing the Balance Equation™, we discovered that "How do I feel?" is one of the most important questions you can ask yourself. If we make the time to reflect on how we feel via the Balance Equation™ instead of simply powering through the day, it's easier to decide what we want to prioritize and include in our routines.

⬤ TBE EXERCISE

Do a Daily Self-Check-in

Ideally, you should do a self-check-in at least once a day or periodically throughout the day by simply asking yourself, "How do I feel?" This habit allows you to be in touch with your feelings, prioritize what's important to you, and move the needle toward that future vision of yourself. Do this with a simple quick scan in the four categories of self, health, relationships, and money. This practice offers a broad view and is a simple way to see if something pops up that needs immediate attention.

If you feel bad about your physical health or have missed doing your exercises the past few days, have self-compassion but realize this means you haven't made exercise a priority. In order to change this reality, consider adding a Micro-move™ to an existing routine or starting a new routine. Perhaps it would help to use the Balance Equation™ assessment for your daily check-ins. Again, you can download it from the QR Code below.

 Open up the camera on your phone and scan the QR code, which will bring you to a menu. Click on "Get Your Balance Number Now!" to take the assessment.

The key is scheduling routine days and times, like we do below, so that you engage in this check-in consistently.

⫶🏃 TBE IN ACTION

Rob's Morning Routine

Rob has been following a morning routine for the past thirty years. It all started during the early development of the Balance Equation™. He wanted to start each day with enthusiasm and a positive attitude that set the table for a good day. He found that he was doing bits and pieces of a morning routine for several years, but he didn't put it all together until ten years ago. Today, his morning routine consists of the following:

1. Awaken at 5:30 a.m.
2. Hit the bathroom to pee, brush his teeth, splash water on his face, and put on his sweats.
3. Mentally assess how he feels physically, mentally, socially, emotionally, and spiritually.
4. Weigh in and check blood pressure to see if his numbers support his mental assessment.
5. Drink his first glass of water.
6. Meditate for three to ten minutes.
7. Practice affirmations, healing breathing, and gratitude for two to five minutes.
8. Read for three to ten minutes.
9. Journal and record his check-in numbers for five to ten minutes.
10. Move and stretch for three to ten minutes.
11. Breakfast for five to fifteen minutes.

Total time: twenty-four to seventy-five minutes depending on how much time he has and how he feels.

Rob explains, "Having a morning routine sets a positive tone for the day because I've accomplished taking care of mind, body, and soul. This routine is part of the self and health categories. Being consistent and getting it done first thing in the day protects me as the day opens up and becomes busy. On a day I'm pressed for time, I still do my routine, but I might cut the time shorter for each Micro-move™. Healing, breathing, and affirmations might last a minute, but even stretching for a minute is better than not stretching at all. Each action can take one minute if I'm pressed for time."

The internal dialogue you should have as you check in with yourself centers on how you feel. Is anything missing or causing stress or anxiety? Rob says, "If the answer is yes, I think further about the cause and what I can do about it. If it's an upcoming due date on a project, I make sure to schedule time the same day to complete the work per the deadline and then I feel better. If I feel down or depressed, I might add more meditation or exercise into my calendar. The act of calendaring is a Micro-move™ that turns my response into routine. The routine might last a day, a week, a month, a year, or it might become a habit. The same dialogue should occur for health, relationships, and money. This isn't a long dialogue. The whole scan and self-talk might last a minute or two max."

Stu's Morning Routine

Stu has been following a morning routine for at least thirty years. It all started during the early development of the Balance Equation™. He wanted to start each day with enthusiasm and

152

a positive attitude that set the table for a good day. He found that he was doing bits and pieces of a morning routine for several years, but it didn't all come together until about fifteen years ago. He follows this routine consistently every day without exception. According to Stu, "Consistency is the key. Skipping it is not an option for me."

Here is Stu's morning routine:

1. Wake up at 5:30 a.m.
2. Weigh himself.
3. Splash water on his face, head, and mouth and use mouthwash.
4. Go to home office.
5. Perform prayer rituals.
6. Pray for all the people in his life.
7. Pray for the day.
8. Set a timer to read for ten minutes.
9. Write one page in a journal.
10. Start taking daily vitamins and medication.
11. Drink water with every pill.
12. Do thirty pushups after the first pill.
13. Do thirty bicep curls.
14. Continue taking vitamins.
15. Open spreadsheet and record any expenses from the day before.
16. Open the bank app and reconcile all balances, including cash on hand.
17. Go downstairs and hit brew on the coffee maker.
18. Pour coffee and reset the machine.
19. Go for a walk while drinking coffee.

Stu notes, "I write my own prayers and affirmations every day. One of them is, 'God, let me react to my wife with only love, care, and respect.' Writing this intention helps me to react only in that way."

Neither Rob nor Stu checks email or watches the news first thing in the morning. This frees up time to check in with their spouses and has been a vital factor in their relationships.

From Micro-move™ to Routine

The importance and benefits of Micro-moves™ have been discussed throughout the book. A mindful self-check-in using the TBE assessment per the QR code below is an example of how to turn a Micro-move™ into a routine. While it only takes one to two minutes to determine how you feel, reviewing the results, comparing it to the Balance Equation™ Community, and deciding on your priorities takes a few minutes longer. However, the benefit of the daily self-check-in is that you're able to prioritize the areas of your life that you want to feel better about. The graphic below the QR code highlights the process.

 Open up the camera on your phone and scan the QR code, which will bring you to a menu. Click on "Get Your Balance Number Now!" to take the assessment.

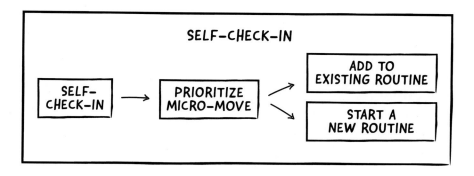

When Do Routines Become Habits?

According to James Clear in *Atomic Habits*, all habits follow a similar trajectory from effortful practice to automatic behavior, a process known as automaticity. Automaticity is the ability to perform a behavior without thinking about each step, which occurs when the non-conscious mind takes over. The key is repetition: the more you practice a behavior, the more ingrained it becomes. Over time, this practice can become a routine.

Your daily routine affects every area of your life in the Balance Equation™: self, health, relationships, and money. Your bedtime and sleep habits affect your performance the next day, including your mental sharpness, emotional well-being, and energy levels. A good routine consists of maintaining a consistent time for waking up in the morning and going to bed. It can start with something small—i.e., a Micro-move™—that grows over time.

Better health is a result of just a little extra planning. Having a routine can help you be productive, get and stay organized, and find passion and meaning in your life. Healthy routines can provide structure, organization, and greatly improve your health, but routines aren't just related to health. Reading for ten minutes is a routine that affects self and development. While the example below is extreme, take a look at actor and businessman Mark Wahlberg's morning routine shared in *Business Insider* on September 12, 2018.

Mark Wahlberg's Typical Daily Routine

- 2:30 a.m.—Wake up
- 2:45 a.m.—Prayer time
- 3:15 a.m.—Breakfast
- 3:40 a.m.—Work out
- 5:30 a.m.—Post-workout meal
- 6:00 a.m.—Shower
- 7:30 a.m.—Golf
- 8:00 a.m.—Snack
- 9:30 a.m.—Cryo chamber (cold immersion, which improves post workout recovery).
- 10:30 a.m.—Snack
- 11:00 a.m.—Family time, meetings, and work calls
- 1:00 p.m.—Lunch
- 2:00 p.m.—Meetings and work calls
- 3:00 p.m.—Pick up kids at school
- 3:30 p.m.—Snack
- 4:00 p.m.—Workout #2
- 5:00 p.m.—Shower
- 5:30 p.m.—Dinner and family time
- 7:30 p.m.—Bedtime

Who has time for this? More power to Mark, who makes time. This may be one of the many reasons he was one of the top grossing male actors in 2020 earning, more than fifty-eight million dollars according to *Forbes*. We can all use a routine, but it doesn't have to be like Rob's, Stu's, or Mark's. Make it your own, have fun with it, and get up every day and try again. A good morning routine will be a great addition to your life that will make your days better.

⫶🏃 TBE IN ACTION

Routine Frequency

Routines don't need to be repeated every day. They can also be repeated weekly, monthly, or annually. For example, Stu has a weekly Sunday routine that includes waking up early and jumping in the car to drive twenty minutes through the canyon for a walk at the Pacific Ocean in Malibu. The steps in his Sunday morning routine include:

- Performing his typical daily morning routine
- Driving to Malibu
- Getting a great cup of coffee
- Sending the same picture every time to his daughter, Abby
- Walking three to six miles depending on how he feels
- Picking up breakfast for his wife, Andrea
- Returning no later than 10:00 a.m.

On Father's Day every year, Stu honors his dad, Larry. He has consistently followed this routine without missing a day since his dad passed away in 1995. Stu's Father's Day routine includes:

- Performing his typical daily morning routine;
- Picking up his dad's favorite sesame bagel;
- Meeting up with his kids;
- Visiting his dad's gravesite;
- Putting the bagel where the flowers usually go (his dad would definitely prefer the bagel); and
- Reflecting, talking to his dad, and praying.

The unexpected benefit of this annual routine is sharing important memories of his dad while spending quality time with his kids.

Routines Can Be Fun

Routines don't have to be dull and boring. In fact, the health benefits you'll reap in all areas of your life will leave you wondering why you didn't create a healthy routine sooner. Here are some of the ongoing benefits of creating a healthy routine:

- **Reduced stress:** a healthy routine can give you more time to relax, help you experience less stress and anxiety, and reduce your risk for developing heart disease, diabetes, or other health issues.
- **Improved sleep:** your quality of sleep is affected by your daily routines and bedtime habits, which affect how you feel the next day, which in turn affect all areas in the Balance Equation™—self, health, relationships, and money.
- **Good health:** if necessary, set your alarm a little earlier each morning so you have time to do healthy things for the body such as hydrate, meditate, exercise, and eat a healthy breakfast, all of which will energize you and help you take on the day.

Healthy routines work well for many people, but everyone is unique. You have to find what works for you, knowing that creating a healthy routine will enhance your health and make you more efficient. Don't try to do everything at once.

● TBE EXERCISE

Create a New Routine

Do you have any routines? What are they? Grab a piece of paper and write down your current routines and current state. Where do you need to improve your current routine or perhaps create a healthier one? Choose one area and create that new routine. Your Micro-move™ might be putting on your sneakers in the morning so it will be easier to take a break from work and go for a walk. If you need to get a better night's sleep, a Micro-move™ would be shutting down all your devices at least an hour before bed, putting a drop of lavender essential oil on your pillow, or enjoying a cup of chamomile tea.

Strive for the Micro-move™ Multiplier, or Triple M

The Micro-move™ multiplier provides a multiplication effect and acceleration to making positive changes in your life. Micro-moves™ are small steps that, added up, become routines and habits. A good example of a Micro-move™ multiplier is having a healthy routine that gives you more confidence and motivates you to make healthy habits part of your morning routine such as combining exercise, prayer, meditation, affirmations, visualization, reading, and journaling. By committing to a new healthy habit, you become more confident about adding another healthy habit, which leads to a more successful and happier you. That's the point of creating healthy routines: you can build on them. Keep them small so you can do them consistently, then grow with them.

When you take a moment to stop and ask yourself, "How am I feeling right now?" you can follow it up with a Micro-move™ to make a change that will help you feel better or enhance your good feelings. The Balance Equation™ assessment takes only a few minutes and can provide you with needed clarity, which also helps build momentum.

Be Consistent

Consistency means doing things that allow you to routinely and regularly practice healthy habits that get you where you want to be. Optimize your Micro-moves™ and be open to change so that your actions fit your life. When you take action to optimize each Micro-move™ and are consistent with that action, you will get better at your routines, which will help you move in the right direction for the ideal you.

Be Reasonable about Your Expectations

It might take time to see the benefits of Micro-moves™, but once you optimize them, you will get better at making time for them or having built-in cushions in case things don't go as planned. A "cushion" means getting up five minutes earlier than you used to so that you have time to meditate or setting your watch five minutes earlier so you're on time for your Zoom meeting. Also be careful about over-scheduling yourself—that's something you definitely want to avoid.

It's *Not* All or Nothing

If you miss a routine, don't beat yourself up. Practice self-compassion and make a promise to do better tomorrow. In fact, under promise and over deliver so you can enjoy your new routines. Managing yourself can be difficult at times because it requires self-discipline. For example, if you get off track by eating an unhealthy meal, forgive yourself and promise to do better at your next meal. Achieving balance isn't a race. It's about continuous improvement and directional movement toward your goals and objectives.

Watch Out for Time Robbers and Time Wasters

Time robbers and time wasters include watching the news, spending time on social media, and surfing the internet. These are great activities if you schedule them, but they're time robbers if they aren't scheduled. Save time by using time savers. For example, if your files aren't in order or your desk is a mess, you can create a routine at the end of your day of clearing or cleaning up your desk—that "time saver" will help you start efficiently tomorrow.

If you're easily distracted, set boundaries for yourself. You might have to set a timer to limit phone calls to five minutes. Letting other people take you off task is a time suck you probably haven't planned for. In addition, it takes a certain amount of time to refocus on the task at hand. You don't have to schedule everything, but do schedule blocks of down time for whatever it is you want to do.

Alan Lakein, author of *How to Get Control of Your Time and Life*, said, "Time equals life; therefore, waste your time and waste your life, or master your time and master your life." Mastering your life means planning or scheduling important things that bring your future into the present moment.

161

Like Lakein, we want you to establish your priorities based on your goals of the ideal you. What do you want to achieve? Think about the Micro-moves™ you can do today, tomorrow, and next week to fulfill those goals. Make the best use of your time by focusing on your priorities. Anything else is a waste of time. Lakein advocates repeating, "I am wasting my time" again and again any time you are doing something besides the priority you have set for yourself. Whatever you're doing might be worthwhile, but that doesn't matter if it takes you away from your highest priority.

Focus on giving your best energy and time to the most important things in your life, and you will end up with a fulfilling life. The many writings of Thich Nhat Hanh, the well-known Vietnamese Buddhist monk, suggest we should relax more and enjoy each activity without wasting time on regret over failures, guilt over things left undone, or the inevitable periods when time is being wasted by things beyond our control. Instead, we should focus on achieving the things that are most important to us.

Boundaries Are Important

It is important to know boundaries, both your boundaries and those of others. This knowledge will allow you to make decisions and keep you from compromising your core values and beliefs. What's more, when you respect others' boundaries, you are making a statement that you understand the importance of their time, their routines, and what is important to them.

One Micro-move™ Affects Another

When developing a routine, remember that a single Micro-move™ in one category of the Balance Equation™ can help you in the other three categories. For example, when you sleep better, you feel and look better the next day. You're rested enough so that you feel like exercising and tackling the projects at work. Your daily routine is a series of Micro-moves™ with a cause and effect that will help you do and feel better, make positive changes, and accomplish your goals. It all goes back to how you feel.

Sometimes You Have to Take a Step Back to Move Forward

This statement might seem counterintuitive, but it's true. Here's how to take a step back in order to move forward:

1. Identify the baggage in your life.
2. Look at how it impacts you.
3. Subtract the baggage that prevents you from moving forward and being happy.

Think through a regular day in your life. As you mentally move through each of your routines, all the way to the end of the day, ask yourself if you're happy. Really think about it. If, after analyzing your day, you feel like you have the potential to be happier, take another step back and think, "What's keeping me from being fully and completely happy?" Maybe it's as small as the mess at your front entryway that has bothered you all week or as big as an addiction. Whatever it is, if it's keeping you from your happily-ever-after at the end of the day, identify it, then take steps to solve it.

Types of Routines

Routines come in all shapes and sizes. While you might initially think routines are boring, they actually save time and brainpower. For example,

163

look at how a healthy morning and evening routine impacts every category of your life:

- **Self:** a healthy morning and evening routine makes good use of time throughout your day more sustainable.
- **Health:** waking up after a good night's sleep, eating a healthy breakfast, getting and staying hydrated, and exercising give you a healthier body and mind.
- **Relationships:** a healthy routine decreases stress and makes you calmer and happier, especially when you give yourself time to meditate, write in your gratitude journal, or exercise.
- **Money:** a healthy daily routine saves you money because healthy habits help prevent illness and/or disease.

Additional Micro-moves™ for creating healthy routines include the following:

- **Wake up at the same time each morning.** An inconsistent sleep schedule can affect your energy levels throughout the day and increase the risk of high blood pressure, heart disease, diabetes, and obesity.
- **Hydrate first thing in the morning.** After a good night's sleep, it's important to hydrate as soon as you wake up. Dehydration can cause fatigue and headaches and make it difficult to concentrate. Keep a water bottle by your bed, or, better yet, squeeze the juice of a fresh lemon into a tall water glass, fill the glass with water, and drink up.
- **Take the time to reflect on the positive.** You can do this by writing in your gratitude journal or simply reflecting on what you're grateful

for as you begin to meditate. This only takes a minute, but it sets a positive tone for the rest of the day.

- **Start with a healthy breakfast.** Think protein and fiber and include some healthy fats. Try nut butter on whole-grain toast with an egg or a protein smoothie made with plain Greek yogurt, organic berries, and a scoop of nut butter. Meals like these will help you load up on nutrient-dense foods that will control hunger all day.

- **Avoid starting the day with news.** Watching the news or checking social media first thing in the morning can overload your mind with negative thoughts. Focus on taking care of yourself first thing in the morning before you delve into the negative events happening in the world.

- **Keep your phone and other electronics out of your bedroom.** Research by the Associated Professional Sleep Societies (APSS) shows that cell phones can disrupt sleep, causing restlessness, stress, and fatigue. One reason could be that cell phones radiate electromagnetic waves into the environment constantly, not just when they're being used. This is why placing your cell phone near your head while you sleep is bad for you. Plus, random text messages or calls can startle you awake, prompt you to respond while you're half asleep, and make it difficult to fall back asleep.

- **Use affirmations.** Write down an affirmation and post it where you'll see it first thing in the morning such as near your coffee cup or on the bathroom mirror. Say it out loud or to yourself. A few examples are, "I am grateful," "Good things will happen today," and "I am great."

- **Get outside.** Natural sunlight affects our melatonin levels and circadian rhythms, which help regulate sleep. Just ten minutes of sunlight a day can decrease your stress levels and boost your mood.

- **Play some good music.** Anything that makes you feel glad or energized is a good choice. You certainly can't go wrong with "Happy" by Pharell Williams. Listen to it while you wash your face, brush your teeth, or take a shower to boost your mood.

- **Start your day with exercise.** This is one of the healthiest habits you can embrace because it will decrease depression, boost your energy, improve your memory, and enhance your overall health. Go for a walk, lift weights, take a yoga class in person or on YouTube, or go for a bike ride. For those interested in losing weight, the *International Journal of Obesity* reports that people who exercise in the morning lose more weight than those who exercise in the evening.

- **Sit still and smiling.** Just five minutes spent sitting still and smiling can stimulate the release of endorphins that make you feel good. You can make smiling part of meditation, which has been proven to lower blood pressure and improve your concentration and focus.

- **Make a plan.** Writing down what you hope to accomplish each day can help you be more productive. Plus, you'll find that you worry less about any unfinished tasks.

- **Do a self-check-in.** How do you feel? How does your body feel? Doing a self-check-in can help you determine what you might need to do next. You can actually do this before getting out of bed each morning.

- **Read a good book.** Instead of checking social media, read a good book. According to the *Journal of Teaching and Learning*, reading helps lower your heart rate and blood pressure by helping you feel more relaxed and less anxious.

- **Use Micro-moves™.** Add one thing to your morning or evening routine. After a week, assess if it's working for you. If it isn't, try something else. For example, if making a morning smoothie in the blender is waking everyone up, go with oatmeal and berries with a scoop of almond butter instead or make your smoothie the night before and store it in the refrigerator.

- **Be prepared.** Anything you can do to prepare for the morning will give you a head start and make your mornings more pleasant. For example, set up the coffee maker the night before and set out your favorite coffee mug so it's ready to go. Make sure you have the ingredients for your smoothie or set out your workout clothes to make it easier to exercise.
- **Be kind to yourself.** It takes time to form healthy habits, so give yourself time to get used to a new routine. Focus on the progress you're making, not on perfection. If the day doesn't go as planned, get back into the groove the next day.

Incorporating regular routines into your daily schedule can help keep your mind and body healthy and running smoothly. Maintaining positive mental and physical health can stabilize your body clock, make you more productive, help you lose weight, make it easier to stay in touch with family and friends, save you money, and, most importantly, help you achieve your priorities and an ideal *you*, so choose a routine to incorporate into your life today, right now.

Winding Down Routine

Now that you have some ideas for a healthy morning routine, let's take a look at some winding down routines. Yes, routines are just as important at the end of the day as they are at the beginning. You might find it difficult to turn off work and switch gears so that you're mentally present at night with your spouse and family, but it's important to be able to switch between work and family life or you'll feel frustrated, tired, or even burned out because you aren't recharging your batteries, having fun, and enjoying the time you're spending with those you care about most. Here are some winding down routines that will help you do just that:

- **Schedule time off.** This means shutting down your computer and turning the office or work area lights off at a scheduled time. Surprisingly, this technique helps you be more productive because you know you only have a certain amount of time to get your work done. As a result, you set better priorities about what needs to be done by the end of the day and what can wait.

- **Create the winding down routine that works for you.** You might need to set a timer to remind yourself to stop work as scheduled. You might prepare for the next day, return any important phone calls or emails, and let some phone calls go to voicemail so you don't start a long conversation that will interfere with your schedule.

- **Clean up your work area.** Tidying up your workspace will help you be ready and organized for tomorrow's workday. Jot down important appointments for the next day, check items off your to-do list, and put files and books back where you got them.

- **Create a transition ritual.** If you drive home, you might listen to music or an audiobook. If possible, you might crack the window and get some fresh air or just enjoy the view. If you work from home, you might turn on some music and enjoy a glass of wine before dinner with your spouse, or perhaps this is your ideal time to get a workout in.

- **Exercise.** Exercise is always a good way to transition after work because it releases stress hormones that build up in your body. Go for a brisk walk, run, ride your bike, and enjoy the natural world around you—it will help you relax.

- **Establish working hours at home.** All work and no play isn't good, and with so many people now working from home, it's even more important to separate work from home as much as possible. Limit "shop talk" and spend quality time with your spouse and family.

🏃 TBE IN ACTION

Rob's Bedtime Routine

Bedtime rituals are also important, and Rob has a ten- to fifteen-minute bedtime routine that sets the tone for a good night's sleep. This practice, which continues to improve, results in more than two hours of REM (healing sleep) sleep every night and consists of the following:

- Turning off all screens (TV, phone, etc.)
- Engaging in deep breathing and meditation
- Saying out loud three things he's grateful for
- Saying out loud three things he accomplished today
- Saying out loud three things he wants to accomplish tomorrow
- Saying out loud three affirmations, such as "I am healthy," "I am safe," and "We have each other's back"
- Engaging in more deep breathing
- Closing his eyes to begin sleep for the night

This routine has worked so well for Rob that his wife, Beth, has joined him in this bedtime practice, which in turn has further enhanced the close relationship between this long-married and devoted pair.

As you can see, it's important to have routines that allow you to focus on your priorities, partner, and family. Routines allow you to schedule time to relax your mind, body, and soul. Look for ways to create an exercise routine, meditation routine, and/or healthy meal routine, then incorporate them into your life.

RECAP

Routines are a critical component of continuous personal improvement within the Balance Equation™. Routines create consistency and repetition that help Micro-moves™ stick. You can attach a Micro-move™ to an existing routine or let a Micro-move™ become its own routine. Either way, the repetition and consistency of routines helps turn them into habits.

According to research from Tel Aviv University, routines are calming and help reduce anxiety. Additional benefits include helping you:

- Control your day
- Maximize your brainpower to engage in important tasks
- Wake up more refreshed
- Improve relationships
- Make more time for the activities you enjoy
- Enjoy better physical and mental health

Ask yourself, "How do I feel?" Consider a self-check-in at least once per day. Automaticity is the ability to perform a behavior without thinking about each step. Over time, with repetition, routines can become habits.

Your TBE Jumpstart

If you can't fly, then run. If you can't run, then walk. If you can't walk, then crawl, but by all means, keep moving.

—Martin Luther King Jr.

Change isn't easy or comfortable. However, feeling better about the life story you're creating requires action and growth. The "F" factor (fun, fear, faith, focus) discussed in chapter eight almost always comes up when people consider adding or subtracting something from their lives. Here's our response: let faith overcome fear and have fun while staying focused on the actions you're taking.

Try to avoid making excuses too. We're all familiar with rhetorical questions such as "Who has time for this?" and phrases like "I'd love to do this but I don't have time." Remember, balance means living a life where all your priorities are reflected by the way you spend your time. Make time for your priorities, and you'll feel better about your life.

If you haven't yet incorporated the Balance Equation™ into your life, you can jumpstart the process right now, for once and for all, by making TBE time and then jumping into the four steps. Here's that QR code again to make it easy to begin.

 Open up the camera on your phone and scan the QR code, which will bring you to a menu. Click on "Get Your Balance Number Now!" to take the assessment.

Now that you're clear on your numbers, schedule a block of time each day for your personal TBE jumpstart. It's important when choosing this time to think about the following:

- **Amount.** To be successful and help ensure consistency, start small, with two to five minutes per day.
- **Frequency.** At least five days a week is a good place to start.
- **When.** Morning, noon, or night or whatever time of day works best for you.

- **Where.** Pick a place that's quiet and comfortable so that you can assess, reflect, and prioritize how you feel about the categories in your life.

With these details clarified, you're ready to jump into the four steps on a daily basis. Just remember that these various elements can be changed as needed to meet your personal needs. The important thing to remember is that we all need consistency and repetition to make change stick.

Step #1: Assess Your Current State

On a daily basis, take two to four minutes to click on the QR code below and take the TBE Assessment. This is the best investment you can make to get a clear picture of how you feel about all the categories in your life.

 Open up the camera on your phone and scan the QR code, which will bring you to a menu. Click on "Get Your Balance Number Now!" to take the assessment.

Step #2: Identify One Category You Want to Improve

Look through the results of your TBE assessment to identify the first category you want to improve. This will likely be one of your lower numbers. If you're so inclined, compare your scores to the Balance Equation™ Community's average scores in the chart below.

The Balance Equation™ (TBE™) Assessment

	YOUR BALANCE #	COMMUNITY AVERAGE
TOTAL	73	74.34
SELF	21	18.69
Core Values & Beliefs	5	4.21
Personal Time	5	3.47
Development	4	3.62
Work	3	3.82
Spiritual	4	3.57
HEALTH	16	18.18
Physical	3	3.67
Mental	4	3.53
Emotional	3	3.80
Food	3	3.66
Sleep	3	3.51
RELATIONSHIPS	20	19.13
Most Significant Other	3	4.02
Family	4	3.77
Friends	4	3.88
Work	3	3.82
Inner Circle	4	3.74
MONEY	16	18.34
Basic Expenses	4	4.07
Debt	4	3.95
Savings	3	3.79
Retirement	2	3.40
Charity	3	3.12

Step #3: Choose One Micro-move™ to Prioritize

Choose a Micro-move™ that resonates with you from the list on pages 120–123.

Step #4: Include the Micro-move™ in Your Life

Nike says, "Just do it." We say, "Just include it" to feel better about your life. Doing so helps you overcome any fear you might feel about trying something new, but there's still that little factor called making it stick.

Make It Stick

How do you make your Micro-moves™ stick? Here's how:

- **Consistency and repetition.** As mentioned in chapter eight, consistency and repetition are key to forming new habits. Once you've determined a Micro-move™ to include in your routine, include it in your schedule to make it stick. Many people try something new once or twice and then give up. Don't do this. Be persistent. It will pay off.
- **Planning and scheduling.** Remember what Ben Franklin said: "If you fail to plan, you are planning to fail." A great quote by motivational speaker Jim Rohn is, "If you don't design your own life plan, chances are you'll fall into someone else's plan. And guess what they have planned for you? Not much." Take matters into your own hands and create a weekly and daily plan. This includes TBE time and Micro-moves™ that will help you be more productive with a plan that works for you. Scheduling your priorities allows you to commit the time you need to achieve your goals. Once you prioritize a Micro-move™ by scheduling a specific time

175

slot, there's a much higher chance you'll complete it. That's why the global task management software market is approaching five billion in annual revenues. We all need tools and systems to keep us on track.

- **Accountability.** As inventor George Washington Carver said, "Ninety-nine percent of all failures come from people who have a habit of making excuses." Most people fail to achieve their goals because they lack self-awareness; there is always someone or something to use as an excuse. How do we hold ourselves accountable so that we achieve our priorities? While planning and scheduling might be enough to make TBE stick for you, finding an accountability partner, coach, or group can be vital. According to a study from the Association for Training and Development, when you commit to someone that you will accomplish a goal, your probability for achievement is sixty-five percent. When you create a specific accountability appointment with a person you're committed to, the odds increase to ninety-five percent in your favor. Simply put, the likelihood of getting new habits to stick dramatically increases when you set a time to report back to someone on your progress.

- **Tracking your success.** It's important to track what is and is not working in any new program or system. Doing so highlights the fact that what gets measured can be moved in the direction you choose. Therefore, we recommend using the TBE assessment daily, weekly, or monthly to see where your number/numbers are. There are many ways to track your progress. You can use a piece of paper, a spreadsheet, or the TBE assessment via the QR code itself. The key is to regularly measure your progress over time.

Expect the Unexpected

Famed University of Alabama coach Bear Bryant was quoted as saying, "Expect the unexpected." As mentioned earlier, the Yiddish phrase is "Mann tracht, und Gott lacht," which means "Man plans and God laughs." You've probably also heard terms such as "best-laid plans," "sh*t happens," and so on.

We are all impacted by things that are out of our control. No matter how we incorporate the Balance Equation™ and planning, scheduling, accountability, and tracking into our lives, we need to be flexible. Life interruptions come in different forms, but one thing is for sure: they will arrive for all of us at different points in time and can be anything from a flat tire to a bad night's sleep, a health issue, a relationship issue, or a money issue. In short, it's reasonable to expect the unexpected.

Rob recently experienced the unexpected with a cancer diagnosis that showed up while writing this book. Thanks to his very supportive co-author, the pair carried on, scheduling around a multitude of doctor appointments. Rob has had the same support from his business partners, Marc and Aaron, and from his wife and family.

RECAP

Our definition of balance is living a life where all your priorities are reflected by the way you spend your time. Make time for your priorities, and you'll feel better about your life. Follow the TBE jumpstart process to do this. Then, once you've made time to take the Balance Equation™ assessment, you can:

Step #1: Assess your current state.
Step #2: Reflect and identify one category you want to
improve.

Step #3: Choose a Micro-move™ to prioritize.
Step #4: Include the Micro-move™ in your life and grow.

Thereafter, you can make the Balance Equation™ stick with:

- Consistency and repetition
- Planning and scheduling
- Accountability
- Tracking

Expect the unexpected. We are all affected by things that are out of our control. No matter how fully and successfully we incorporate the Balance Equation™ into our lives, we need to be flexible.

Conclusion

This program is useless without action. Don't wait to start prioritizing what is most important to you. We didn't write this book for ourselves. We wrote it to help you better manage and consequently feel better about all areas of your life, from self to health to relationships to money. We hope you've learned the importance of frequently assessing your self, your health, your relationships, and your money to get a quick snapshot of how you feel at any given moment in time. Hopefully, you will reflect on the areas you want to prioritize, then add Micro-moves™ to improve your life.

As mentioned in the introduction, a small change today has an exponential effect on how your future plays out. Utilizing the Balance Equation™ and realizing the positive changes that can occur will amaze you. The more you do it, the better you'll feel because you'll be able to live your life while prioritizing what is most important to you.

We all sometimes feel unmotivated. When this happens, grab this book, get fired up, and never forget Anthony Bourdain's haunting words:

"Balance? I fu*king wish." Instead, let's live like Aunt Gertie, with minimal regrets and abundant richness, and let's get started now.

A portion of the proceeds from each copy of *The Balance Equation*™ will be donated to the American Foundation for Suicide Prevention. For more information, visit *www.afsp.org*. It is our hope that all people in need along with their families and friends will take advantage of this great resource.

Acknowledgments

Many people have added to our life experiences and consequently enhanced this book. There are too many to mention, so if anyone feels left out, please accept our sincere apologies.

With that, fist pumps and elbow knocks to each other for completing this book during the never-ending COVID-19 pandemic. Writing this book took four plus years of meeting almost every Saturday at the local library until it closed in March of 2020 followed by Zoom meetings and many other dedicated evenings, weekends, and writing retreats while balancing full-time jobs and busy lives. We estimate that it took more than 3,300 cups of home-brewed coffee (with a savings of almost $15,000 per chapter six), more than 100,000 ounces of water, lots of snacks, countless walks around the block, and many meditation and bathroom breaks to complete the task.

Thank you to our amazing team of contributors: Alan Berkowitz, Annie Hyman-Pratt, April McNally, Arlene Dorn, Barry London, Beth Fiance, Dan Habecker, Bill Hawfield, Camille Taub, Diedre Johnson, Garrett Rosenblum, Gertrude "Aunt Gertie" Drucker, Izzy Grimaldi, Jeff Broudy, Reid Broudy, Wendy Broudy, Jerry Drucker, Joshua Taub, Marc Netka, Marie Ward, Max Gaynes, Miguel Andorfy and the MeSalva team, Nick "Keke" Campillo, Ron Miller and his UCLA MBA students, Sherry Granader, Sophia Gaynes, Susan Barnett, the team at Jenkins Group (Jerry Jenkins, Jim Kalajian, Leah Nicholson, Yvonne Roehler, and Rebecca Chown), and the Sky High team. Your hard work and dedication helped make our vision a reality.

Thank you also to our partners, coworkers, business associates, and mentors: Aaron Toczynski, Al Watt, Alan Berkowitz, Alex Inman, Andy Byer, Barry London, Bill Hawfield, Brian Adams, Bryan Shark, Christine Anderson, Clark Buch, Claudia Kananen, Coach Burdon, Coach Casey,

Coach Greene, The UCSB Lacrosse (undefeated 1980 champions), Dennis Fortner, DeShaunda Gooden-Warner, Gail Boudreaux, Garrett Semola, Gloria McCarthy, Great Neck North (undefeated 1976 champions), Greg Antoniono, Jim Ardell, Mallory Follmer, Marc Netka, Mark Dorner, Rabbi Shlomo Bistritzky, Rabbi Yitzchak Sapochkinsky, Rejeev Ronanki, Shane O'Reilly, Steve Omlor, Team ASA, Team EHSA, Team Awesome, and the Sockem Dogs (Annie Hyman-Pratt, Brett Dillenberg, Ken Gootnick, Ron Miller, Mark Brown, Ron Greitzer, Frank Nemiroff, Steve Phillips, Jeff Marks, Greg Yost, and Jim Weldon). Your leadership and wisdom inspired us and made us better people.

Thank you also to our families and extended families: Al and Sylvia Rosenblum, Art and Gloria Schimmel, Christie Schimmel, Gertrude Drucker, Jeff Rosenblum, Keith and Jody Lopaty, Lisa Rubenstein, Mini Levine, Neil Schimmel, the Broudys, the Cohens, the Druckers, the Elkins, the Feinbergs, the Fiances, the Friedlands, the Furas, the Habeckers, the Katzmans, the Kupermans, the Levines, the Lopatys, the Malkins, the Newmans, the Rosenblums, the Rowans, the Rubensteins, the Schimmels, the Taubs, and the Wirhts. We are blessed by our shared experiences and your continued unwavering support.

To our parents, Leonard Rosenblum, Sandra Rosenblum, Libby and Seymour Fiance, and Sandra and Herman Cohen, thank you for the gift of life and for providing a strong foundation for our growth.

To our kids and grandkids, Andrew, Amy, Garrett, Virginia, Abby, Wesley, Alex, Kelly, Jeremy, Talia, and Ruby, we love you very much and wish you long and balanced lives.

Finally, to our better halves, Andrea and Beth, thank you for all your encouragement and for sacrificing all those Saturdays and other writing days. We love and appreciate you. Thank you for making us better every day.

Notes

Preface

Hagey, Keach, and Melanie Grayce West. "Anthony Bourdain, CNN TV Host, Is Found Dead in Apparent Suicide." *The Wall Street Journal*.

Dow Jones & Company, June 8, 2018. https://www.wsj.com/articles/anthony-bourdain-cnn-tv-host-is-found-dead-1528458689.

Chapter One: Why the Balance Equation™

Jobs, Steve. "Steve Jobs' 2005 Stanford Commencement Address" (speech, Palo Alto, CA, June 12, 2005). *Stanford News*. https://news.stanford.edu/2005/06/14/jobs-061505/.

Miller, Bennett, director. *Moneyball*. Columbia Pictures, 2011. 2 hrs., 13 min. https://www.netflix.com/title/70201437.

Chapter Two: An Introduction to Micro-moves™

Chapter Three: A Deep Dive into Self

Allen, David. *Getting Things Done: The Art of Stress-Free Productivity*. Penguin, 2015.

Covey, Stephen R. *The 7 Habits of Highly Effective People*. Provo, UT: Franklin Covey, 1998.

Frankl, Viktor E. *Man's Search for Meaning: The Classic Tribute to Hope from the Holocaust*. London: Rider, 2021.

Mcleod, Saul. "Maslow's Hierarchy of Needs." *Simply Psychology*. December 29, 2020. https://www.simplypsychology.org/maslow.html.

Chapter Four: A Deep Dive into Health

World Health Organization. "Mental Health: Strengthening Our Response." World Health Organization. March 30, 2018. https://www.who.int/news-room/fact-sheets/detail/mental-health-strengthening-our-response.

Sawhney, Vasundhara. "It's Okay to Not Be Okay." *Harvard Business Review*. November 10, 2020. https://hbr.org/2020/11/its-okay-to-not-be-okay.

Mineo, Liz. "Over Nearly 80 Years, Harvard Study Has Been Showing How to Live a Healthy and Happy Life." *Harvard Gazette*. November 26, 2018. https://news.harvard.edu/gazette/story/2017/04/over-nearly-80-years-harvard-study-has-been-showing-how-to-live-a-healthy-and-happy-life/.

Coyne, James C., Michael J. Rohrbaugh, Varda Shoham, John S. Sonnega, John M. Nicklas, and James A. Cranford. "Prognostic Importance of Marital Quality for Survival of Congestive Heart Failure." *The American Journal of Cardiology* 88, no. 5 (2001): 526–29. https://doi.org/10.1016/s0002-9149(01)01731-3.

Heller, Daniel, David Watson, and Remus Ilies. "The Role of Person versus Situation in Life Satisfaction: A Critical Examination." *Psychological Bulletin* 130, no. 4 (2004): 574–600. https://doi.org/10.1037/0033-2909.130.4.574.

Staff, Mayo Clinic. "How Much Water Do You Need to Stay Healthy?" Mayo Clinic. Mayo Foundation for Medical Education and Research, October 14, 2020. https://www.mayoclinic.org/

healthy-lifestyle/nutrition-and-healthy-eating/in-depth/water/art-20044256#:~:text=About%2015.5%20cups%20(3.7%20liters, fluids%20a%20day%20for%20women.

Barnes, Christopher M. "Sleep Better, Lead Better." *Harvard Business Review*. August 30, 2018. https://hbr.org/2018/09/sleep-well-lead-better.

Staff, CDC. "CDC—How Much Sleep Do I Need?—Sleep and Sleep Disorders." Centers for Disease Control and Prevention. March 2, 2017. https://www.cdc.gov/sleep/about_sleep/how_much_sleep.html.

Chapter Five: A Deep Dive into Relationships

Zemeckis, Robert, director. *Cast Away*. Image Movers, Playtone, 2000. 2h 24m.

Johnson, Teddi Dineley. "Healthy Relationships Lead to Better Lives." *The Nation's Health*. American Public Health Association, March 1, 2011. https://www.thenationshealth.org/content/41/2/20.

Brooks, Arthur C. "The Seven Habits That Lead to Happiness in Old Age." *The Atlantic*. 2022. https://apple.news/AdjanG2BHRe27UvPqan7v-Q.

Routledge, Clay. *Nostalgia: A Psychological Resource*. New York, NY: Psychology Press, 2016.

Staff, Mayo Clinic. "Friendships: Enrich Your Life and Improve Your Health." Mayo Clinic. *Mayo Healthy Lifestyle Adult Health*, January 12, 2022. https://www.mayoclinic.org/healthy-lifestyle/adult-health/in-depth/friendships/art-20044860.

Chapter Six: A Deep Dive into Money

White, Alexandria. "90% Of Americans Say Money Impacts Their Stress Level, According to New 'Thriving Wallet' Study by Thrive Global and Discover." CNBC. CNBC, November 1, 2021. https://www.cnbc.com/select/why-americans-are-stressed-about-money/.

Gregoire, Carolyn. "How Money Changes the Way You Think and Feel." *Greater Good*, February 8, 2018. https://greatergood.berkeley.edu/article/item/how_money_changes_the_way_you_think_and_feel.

Schwab, Charles. "Schwab Modern Wealth Index Survey 2019." Schwab Brokerage. Charles Schwab, 2019. https://www.aboutschwab.com/modernwealth2019.

Staff, The Ascent. "How Much Time Does the Average American Spend on Personal Finance?" *The Ascent* by The Motley Fool, October 11, 2019. https://www.fool.com/the-ascent/research/average-american-time-personal-finance/.

Huddleston, Cameron. "Survey: 69% of Americans Have Less than $1,000 in Savings." GOBankingRates, December 16, 2019. https://www.gobankingrates.com/banking/savings-account/americans-have-less-than-1000-in-savings/.

Ziv, Shahar. "Which Would You Pick: $1,000,000 or a Magical Penny?" *Forbes Magazine*, July 30, 2019. https://www.forbes.com/sites/shaharziv/2019/07/30/can-you-correctly-answer-the-magical-penny-question/?sh=146c44811a64.

Mutual, Northwestern. "Planning & Progress Study 2019." Newsroom | Northwestern Mutual, 2019. https://news.northwesternmutual.com/planning-and-progress-2019.

Brandon, Emily. "How Much You Will Get from Social Security—US News Money." usnews.com, December 20, 2021. https://money.usnews.com/money/retirement/social-security/articles/how-much-you-will-get-from-social-security.

Oluboba, Silvia. "Why Does Giving Make You Happy (with Real-Life Examples)." *Tracking Happiness*. October 26, 2021. https://www.trackinghappiness.com/why-giving-makes-you-happy/#:~:text=There%20is%20a%20lot%20of,pressure%2C%20and%20even%20better%20longevity.&text=We'll%20also%20tell%20you,to%20be%20a%20happier%20person.

Moll, J., F. Krueger, R. Zahn, M. Pardini, R. de Oliveira-Souza, and J. Grafman. "Human Fronto-Mesolimbic Networks Guide Decisions about Charitable Donation." *Proceedings of the National Academy of Sciences* 103, no. 42 (2006): 15623–28. https://doi.org/10.1073/pnas.0604475103.

Chapter Seven: Moving Your Overall Number with Micro-moves™

Chapter Eight: Accelerating Your Growth and Getting to Flow

Staff, The Ascent. "How Much Time Does the Average American Spend on Personal Finance?" *The Ascent* by The Motley Fool, October 11, 2019. https://www.fool.com/the-ascent/research/average-american-time-personal-finance/.

Frankl, Viktor E. *Man's Search for Meaning*. London, England: Rider, 2021.

Hill, Napoleon. *Think & Grow Rich*. Shippensburg, PA: Sound Wisdom, 2010.

Malin, Jonah. "Why Multitasking Is a Myth, Backed by Science." *The Ladders*. February 3, 2020. https://www.theladders.com/career-advice/why-multitasking-is-a-myth-backed-by-science.

Keller, Gary, and Jay Papasan. *The One Thing: The Surprisingly Simple Truth behind Extraordinary Results*. Austin, TX: Bard Press, 2012.

Foroux, Darius. "Procrastination Study." Darius Foroux, December 31, 2020. https://dariusforoux.com/procrastination-study/.

Glare, P. G. W. *Oxford Latin Dictionary*. Oxford, England: Clarendon Press, 2010.

Geirland, John. "Go with the Flow." *Wired*. Conde Nast, September 1, 1996. https://www.wired.com/1996/09/czik/.

"Flow—The Ultimate State of Being." *Think. Live. Be . . . Positive*. October 8, 2018. https://thinklivebepositive.wordpress.com/2018/10/08/flow-the-ultimate-state-of-being/.

Chapter Nine: TBE Routines

Silva-Jelly, Natasha. "A Day in the Life of Oprah." *Harper's Bazaar*. November 2, 2021.

Ferriss, Timothy. *The 4-Hour Workweek: Escape 9-5, Live Anywhere, and Join the New Rich*. New York, NY: Harmony Books, 2012.

Unnamed. "Keep up with Your Daily Routines for Improved Mental Health." Acenda, March 15, 2021. https://acendahealth.org/blog/keep-up-daily-routines#:~:text=According%20to%20a%20study%2by,and%2520subsequently%252C%2520your%2520life.%2522."and%20subsequently%2C%20your%20life.%22and%2520subsequently%52C%2520your%2520life.%2522.". and%2520subsequently%252C%2520your%2520life.%2522."

Clear, Mark. *Atomic Habits: Let's Change Your Atomic Habits!: A Full Simple Guide to Break Your Bad Routines and Learn New Good Ones.* North Charleston, SC: CreateSpace, 2021.

Shamsian, Jacob. "People Are Creating Their Own Hilarious Daily Schedules after Mark Wahlberg Said He Wakes up at 2:30 A.M. and Spends 1 Hour in 'Cryo Chamber Recovery' Every Day." *Insider*, September 13, 2018. https://www.insider.com/mark-wahlberg-daily-schedule-inspires-fake-schedule-meme-2018-9.

Lakein, Alan. *How to Get Control of Your Time and Life.* New York, NY: Signet Book, 1973.

Willis, E. A., Creasy, S. A., Honas, J. J. et al. "The Effects of Exercise Session Timing on Weight Loss and Components of Energy Balance: Midwest Exercise Trial 2." Int J. Obes 44, 114–124 (2020). https://doi.org/10.1038/s41366-019-0409-x.

Chapter Ten: Your TBE Jumpstart

Vailsher, Lionel Sujay. "Task Management Software Market Revenue Forecast Worldwide 2018–2023." *Statista*. February 22, 2022. https://www.statista.com/statistics/947724/worldwide-task-management-software-market-revenue/.

About the Authors

STUART ROSENBLUM is a serial entrepreneur, business executive, author, and co-founder of the Balance Equation™. Stu is an innovator of new products, services, and business models across many industries, including healthcare, emerging digital technologies, retail, and food service, and has held a wide variety of positions throughout his career, including CEO, president, CFO, and an advisor to CEOs and founders. He has also successfully started, built, and exited several companies, including a restaurant chain that was conceptualized in his home kitchen. As an intrapreneur (an employee who develops an innovative idea within a company and can draw on its resources to do so), Stu created, built, and operated a profitable start-up within a Fortune 20 company with 2021 revenues of $139 billion. In addition to holding degrees in accounting and finance, he passed the CPA exam, acquired his real estate broker's license, and is a certified professional in supply management.

After nearly two decades of working sixty- to eighty-hour weeks, driving long commutes, and putting out fire after fire, Stu examined his life and saw an opportunity to make a shift. A lifelong health and wellness advocate and practitioner in his own life, Stuart teamed up with Rob Fiance to develop The Balance Equation™ and their proprietary Micro-moves™ framework. Change was hard, but Stu steadily improved his life by developing small but powerful daily habits. With the Micro-moves™ framework, Stuart has lost more than eighty pounds, improved his health, transformed his marriage, and cultivated financial security for himself and his family.

Today he thrives in his relationships, health, finances, and senior executive role at a Fortune 20 company by practicing his own Balance Equation™

every day. A world traveler and coach to people of all ages, he enjoys hiking at the beach and spending time with his wife, three grown children, grandchildren, closest friends, and dog, Auggie. Most of all, Stu never stops learning and growing.

ROB FIANCE has practiced health and wellness for more than forty-five years and has incorporated the principles of the Balance Equation™ for the past thirty years. A devoted husband, father, grandfather, author, and co-founder of the Balance Equation™, he is also an experienced board member and C-level executive with a strong track record in pivoting and growing Educational Technology and Health Technology companies. Currently, Rob is COO and partner of STS education, a $120-million edtech company, and a founder and partner of The Healthy Software Company. He is an expert in raising capital, as well as mergers and acquisitions of all sizes, including exits for companies that he has owned.

Rob believes in giving back to his community, particularly in the areas of youth sports. He is a founding member of the Conejo Valley Lacrosse Association and was also a member of the Southern California Lacrosse Association, which launched boys' and girls' high school Varsity Lacrosse in the Conejo Valley and the Tri-County area of Southern California, respectively. Rob has coached hundreds of kids with great success in Agoura High School boys' and girls' Lacrosse teams, winning multiple championships along the way. He is also a member of the University of California Santa Barbara Lacrosse Hall of Fame.

Rob continues to be a mentor in the Kairos Society for CEOs of emerging and growth companies as well as a member of the Sockem Dogs CEO Advisory Group. His specialties include education (both post-secondary and K–12 companies), eLearning, software, technology, healthcare, family businesses, and international partnerships and distribution. He has a Bachelor of Arts degree from the University of California Santa Barbara, and an MBA from UCLA. He is also a Certified Exit Planning Advisor (CEPA) and a Certified Mergers and Acquisitions Advisor (CMAA).

Happily married for more than thirty-six years, Rob has three successful adult children and one grandchild. Above all, Rob is devoted to practicing balance by maintaining his own Balance Equation™ so that he can continue to live his best possible life.

Website and Social Media

For more information, visit Stu's and Rob's website at https://www.thebalanceequation.com.